THE STOCKMEN

THE MAKING OF
AN AUSTRALIAN LEGEND

THE STOCKMEN

THE MAKING OF AN AUSTRALIAN LEGEND

EVAN McHUGH

TO EVERYONE WHO SHARED
THEIR STORIES

CONTENTS

Cattle of the Inland, poster,
c.1930s, James Northfield
(1887–1973).

PROLOGUE

The image of the stockman, a solitary figure etched against an unforgiving landscape, has long been a cornerstone of the Australian character. Despite Australia now being a nation with a predominantly urban population, the notion of a lifestyle in which far horizons set no boundaries and where individual resourcefulness and resilience are challenged on a daily basis remains a deep-rooted part of what it means to be Australian. It's the best qualities of the stockmen and women that we aspire to and are inspired by.

Over the last decade, it's been my privilege to draw together many stories of the outback and bush. Through several books the story of the stockmen has been a thread that weaves in and out of nearly every narrative. Sometimes they've taken centre stage. More often they've been a background presence, quietly getting on with the job while dramatic events unfolded around them. In a land of incredible extremes, they've faced perishing thirst in the arid 'dead heart' of central Australia. They've climbed steep and narrow tracks into the High Country to find summer pasture for cattle and sheep, while risking snowstorms that could sweep down without warning. They've crossed the entire continent with immense herds, traversing some of the loneliest places on Earth.

The opportunity to draw all the stockmen's adventures together and celebrate them in word and image was too good to miss. It's a compelling tale, one that mixes triumph and tragedy, blood, sweat and steers. It extends from the hapless convicts of the First Fleet to the highly skilled mustering pilots of today. It embraces men and women of every race, religion and creed, for there has always been something truly democratic about the life of a stockman. It doesn't matter who you are; it's how good you are that's important.

Stockman and drover Harry Zigenbine, father of Edna Zigenbine, the first woman boss drover, with soldiers at Elliott Bore in 1943.
(State Library of Victoria, H99.201/3147)

Stockmen at full gallop mustering brumbies in the alpine country of New South Wales in 1949. The best brumbies were crossed with domestic horses to produce offspring with great stamina.
(J. Fitzpatrick, National Archives of Australia, A1200, L11971)

Turning A Straggler, wood engraving, 1882, by S. Bennett, captures the danger and challenge of cattle unused to regular handling, especially when their horns were allowed to fully grow.
(State Library of Victoria, IAN05/08/82/sup)

As the experience of stockmen becomes increasingly distant to those who dwell in the urban world, it's easy to romanticise their lives. The positive aspects readily stand out – horsemanship, freedom and friendship among them. However, sit down for a yarn with an old stockman and he'll recall the hardships – long, lonely journeys through dust, rain and cold, a job fraught with danger and sheer hard work.

From the first stockmen chasing cattle on foot and fighting off bushrangers, to those who traded their stockwhips for rifles as they rode to defend their country in foreign battlefields, and on to the modern incarnation aloft in helicopters or launching motorcycles over a sand dune, the stockman has evolved almost beyond recognition. And yet the core qualities remain unchanged. They deal with any challenge that confronts them; they never give up. These are the attributes of stockmen in particular, and through them, Australia as a whole. It's what made us who we are.

Part legend, part hero, an inspiring, charismatic figure, he's a knight in shining armour stripped to the essentials – an adventurous, confident, unpretentious symbol that is the pride of the nation.

FERGUSSON & MITCHELL, IMP.

THE FIRST STOCKMEN

The raw material for the creation of a legend was hard to come by when the First Fleet landed in Sydney Cove in January 1788. Few among the 1332 convicts and guards who disembarked at Port Jackson knew anything about even basic agriculture, let alone handling stock. That much was soon apparent to the Governor of New South Wales, Arthur Phillip, who wrote in a report to Under-Secretary Nepean in July 1788:

> If fifty farmers were sent out with their families they would do more in one year in rendering this colony independent of the mother country as to provisions than a thousand convicts.

In the same report he added:

> The greatest part of the stock brought from the Cape [in South Africa] is dead, and from the inattention of the men who had the care of the cattle, those belonging to Government and two cows belonging to myself are lost. As they have been missing three weeks, it is probable they are killed by the natives. All my sheep are dead and a few only remain of those purchased for Government.

The cattle that escaped comprised one or two bulls, four or five cows, and perhaps a heifer (accounts vary). While Phillip thought the blame lay with the men who were tending the cattle, another convict, Edward Corbett, who had escaped from the settlement at about the same time, was suspected of driving the cattle off in an attempt to supply himself with food. He was later caught and executed.

A concerted effort was made to search for the cattle, whose value to the starving colonists couldn't be overestimated, but there was no sign of the beasts. None of the accounts of the time noted that the search was hampered by a lack of horses, and there were no skilled trackers who could follow what was almost certainly an easily discernible trail.

The hapless convicts, most of them urban poor with no concept of how to handle stock, had been trying to manage the big-boned, broad-horned, bad-tempered Cape cattle on foot and without the benefit of fenced pastures. They may not have realised that the cattle were losing condition on the poor-quality grazing around Sydney Cove. (This lack of nutritious feed was probably what killed the governor's sheep.) When the hungry cattle caught a scent of better pastures elsewhere, nothing could hold them.

It wasn't until seven years later, in 1795, that the fate of the escaped cattle was discovered. Aboriginal people travelling to tribal ceremonies around Sydney reported seeing large beasts in the 'outback', the wild country beyond

Previous spread:
The Cowpastures, engraving, c.1874, Arthur Wilmore (1814–1888) and John Skinner Prout (1805–1876), rich grazing lands to Sydney's south-west to which cattle that escaped from the First Fleet settlers found their way.
(National Library of Australia, an7372821)

A Stockman's Hut, lithograph, 1856, Samuel Thomas Gill (1818–1880). Painted in Australia's early years, it still incorporates an Indigenous Australian and a working dog as elements of the stockman story. Other works by Gill show Aboriginal stockmen doing most of the work while the white stockmen took it easy.
(National Library of Australia, an7178362)

Cattle Branding, lithograph, 1853–1874, Samuel Thomas Gill (1818–1880), demonstrates a stock handling technique that puts both stock and stockmen at risk of severe injury. Modern stock crushes immobilise animals, reducing the chances of harm to all concerned.
(State Library of NSW, a1833038)

the settlements to the south-west of the colony. Then two convicts claimed they'd seen a herd of cattle on the verdant floodplains of the Nepean River, while on a hunting expedition. The then governor, John Hunter, decided to see for himself. Unfortunately, the cattle were completely wild and the governor's party was, as he put it, 'attacked most furiously by a large and very fierce Bull, which rendered it necessary for our own Safety, to fire at him. Such was his Violence and Strength, that six Balls were fired through, before any Person dared approach him.'

Governor Hunter declared that the cattle should be left alone so 'they may become hereafter a very great Advantage and Resource to this Colony'. The reality was that the cattle had staked a claim to the best grazing in the vicinity of Sydney, in an area that came to be known as Cowpastures (now Camden), and the governor lacked the horses and experienced stockmen to argue with them. Meanwhile, the livestock became a 'great advantage and resource' to escaped convicts and the Aboriginal population that was doing battle with the invading English settlers.

Left to its own devices, the herd went forth and multiplied. In 1796 there were estimated to be ninety-four cattle at Cowpastures, but soon they doubled in number, then doubled again. As their numbers grew, some wandered further afield in search of pastures new. In fact, the cattle were pioneering the first of Australia's great stock routes – from Sydney to what would be, in years to follow, the city of Melbourne.

In November 1802, explorer Francis Barrallier revisited the Cowpastures area, and later wrote:

> After half-an-hour's walk we entered a valley where there was a herd of wild cattle. I counted 162 of them peaceably pasturing; they only perceived my party when it was a short distance from them. The cattle advanced several times, as if they were going to attack us, and I had the greatest difficulty in making them leave the place and allow my party to pass. I had even to send my men to pursue them, uttering loud shouts … At a short distance from that place I made my small troop halt, and went alone to the top of a hill to reconnoitre the surrounding country. After walking some 300 paces, on the summit I saw another herd, which I judged was mainly composed of cows and their calves. I was able to count 221 of them, but from the spot where I was it was impossible for me to see them all, and I could only surmise from the lowings, which I heard from various distances, that the number of these cattle must have been very considerable.

While he was there, Barrallier encountered three convicts who had been sent to try and catch some of the wild cattle. The men, on foot, were planning

to set traps. Wrote Barrallier: 'The Governor had promised these men great encouragements if they succeeded.'

It would have been helpful if he'd given them some horses. However, Governor King was a naval man to whom the notion of mustering would have been a complete mystery. It didn't go well for the governor's men. On 5 December, Barrallier wrote:

> The men who had been sent to try and catch the cattle, and who had left here early in the morning, returned in the evening very tired and unsuccessful.

Other convicts who were assigned to work as stockmen had more to contend with than rambunctious ruminants. The trackless depths of the bushland round the first settlements were soon infested with bushrangers, who emerged from their well-concealed hideouts to plunder or disperse flocks and herds, and set fire to the fields and buildings of tyrannical masters.

During November 1806 five escaped convicts had been bushranging together around Prospect Hill, between Sydney and Penrith. They appeared to be targeting the flock of prominent grazier John Macarthur, who lost five sheep in one night. The huts of his shepherds had also been robbed. Macarthur increased the number of shepherds and stationed them on guard at night. Two of them, John Griffiths and an old man named Simeon Donnally were on watch during the night of 8 November 1806 when their sheep started running about within their fold. Bushrangers! According to the *Sydney Gazette* of 16 November 1806:

> Griffiths posted his brother watchman as advantageously as possible, while he himself should reconnoitre, as well as the extreme darkness of the night admitted, the movements of their adversaries. No sooner had they separated than Donnally from some unaccountable cause, forsook his post, and went within the fold, not improbably to discover whether any person had introduced himself therein or not. The other, having traversed a considerable part of the circuit, at length descried a human form, and could not possibly suppose it to be any other than a bushranger. He hailed him instantly, and thrice repeated the challenge; but receiving no answer fired upon him, and the charge having taken place he very soon discovered the object of his aim to have been no other than the unfortunate Donnally, who was mortally wounded in the side.

Donnally, it was revealed at the inquest into his death, was partially deaf and didn't hear Griffiths challenging him. It turned out Griffiths and Donnally were good friends, and while Griffiths wasn't held to account for what had happened, he would forever have the blood of an innocent man on his hands.

Some of the miscreants were brought to justice soon after. While bushrangers tried to provoke Aboriginal people to attack settlers and thereby cause security forces to be diluted, settlers were also trying to enlist Aboriginal people to pursue the bushrangers. With the assistance of one of them, three stockmen tracked the bushrangers to a camp where they were happily dining on a variety of meats, washed down with tea.

Despite being outnumbered, the stockmen rushed them. Given the possibility of a pardon for the convict stockmen if they managed to secure even one bushranger, it was a fight for liberty on both sides. On this occasion the stockmen (and quite probably the tracker) managed to take all six bushrangers prisoner. However, when one of the stockmen went to get some stringy bark with which to tie them up, the bushrangers attacked the remaining two. The stockmen fought hard until their mate returned, whereupon four of the bushrangers escaped, leaving two – named Cox and Halfpenny – too badly knocked about to run. The others, three of them injured to varying degrees, were captured not long after. On 30 November the *Sydney Gazette* reported:

> Patrick Cox [one of the bushrangers] admitted Evidence for the Crown, gave a testimony by which all the parties were criminated. The Court cleared, and after much deliberation returned a Verdict: All guilty – Death.

In December Halfpenny and his brother were executed. Gorman, Kelly and Sheedy had their sentences commuted to transportation for life (meaning they were to remain convicts in Australia for their whole lives, as opposed to those transported to Australia for seven or fourteen years), while Cox was pardoned for informing on the others.

While the early days of stockmen in Australia were inauspicious, it wouldn't be long before capable convicts and free settlers stepped forward to demonstrate the skills that would make stockmen famous. When they did, they reshaped, with extraordinary rapidity, much of the Australian landscape.

THE OVERLANDERS

While the first Europeans in Australia rarely ventured far beyond the settled areas around Sydney, the same couldn't be said of the pioneering cattle, which used Cowpastures as their launchpad into the interior. They did so more than twenty years before a route was 'discovered' over the Blue Mountains, west of Sydney. In doing so they weren't constrained by the early governors of New South Wales, prison wardens in all but name, who feared an exodus of convicts to the greener pastures to the south-west and so forbade any settlement beyond the Nepean River.

It wasn't until wealthy landowners sought to expand their interests and the population had grown that the pressure to extend settlement beyond the Nepean led to confrontations with the autocratic governors. Land grants were made to men such as John Macarthur at Cowpastures as early as 1803, but the landowners' eyes were already looking further afield. Stockyards may have been built at Picton, 15 kilometres south of the Nepean, as early as 1805. Within a few years, squatters were pioneering far beyond the gazetted settlements. By the mid-1820s they'd reached as far as present-day Canberra. A year after the establishment of Melbourne, in 1835, a settlement at Adelaide was begun.

Not surprisingly, graziers were tempted to send livestock south through 'no man's land' to the potential markets in the new settlements, and to stock new stations that were there for anyone bold enough to seize the land from its Indigenous inhabitants. Soon a new breed of pioneering stockman was venturing beyond the fringes of civilisation, heading into the great unknown to drove mobs of cattle and sheep to the fledgling communities. The scanty information about the country ahead of them came only from the sketchy reports of explorers. They made up for it with their own resourcefulness and bush skills, and a healthy dose of courage. They soon became known as The Overlanders.

Next morning I counted the cattle,
Saw the outfit ready to start.
Saw all the lads well mounted,
And their swags put in a cart.
All kinds of men I had
From Germany, France and Flanders;
Lawyers, doctors, good and bad,
In the mob of overlanders.

Anon, 'The Overlanders'

Previous spread:
Droving bullocks in the Northern Territory, 1954. Moving cattle overland, especially where stock routes were yet to be established, involved a constant challenge to find sufficient feed and water to keep stock in good condition.
(Neil Murray, National Archives of Australia, A1200, L17468))

High country beef on the road home from their summer pastures in Victoria, 1966. To most motorists it may seem odd that cattle are allowed to use rural roads. In fact, many of the roads were originally stock routes.
(Keith Byron, National Archives of Australia, A1200, L55192)

The first of them was an Englishman, Joseph Hawdon, who took 300 cattle to Melbourne in 1836, in company with a Hobart banker named John Gardiner and a sea captain called John Hepburn. Regrettably, Hawdon kept no account of his historic trip, and only briefly referred to it in the journal he kept while overlanding cattle from Melbourne to Adelaide in 1838.

> The example of my success led the way to so extensive an emigration from the elder districts of the Colony, that within the last eighteen months there have been taken overland about five thousand head of horned cattle and about one hundred and fifty thousand sheep.

Close behind Joseph was another Englishman, Alexander Fullerton Mollison, who wrote the earliest detailed account of the journey from New South Wales to Port Phillip. He set out in April 1837, leaving Uriara Station (now Uriarra), near Canberra, with approximately 5000 sheep, 600 or 634 cattle (accounts vary), twenty-eight or forty bullocks, twenty-two horses and thirty mostly convict men (some accounts erroneously refer to forty-five men). In addition, he was accompanied by an overseer named Donald McLean and three Aboriginal stockmen, referred to as 'native boys'. His 'plant' – the equipment and horses used for overlanding – included four bullock drays and two horse drays.

His journey was anything but straightforward. Among his many trials, at Gundagai he found it necessary to cross the south-westward-flowing Murrumbidgee River. In Alexander's day there was no bridge, so he sought a ford shallow enough for his entourage and menagerie to cross. The cattle swam the strongly flowing current but things weren't so easy for the sheep. After a couple of days spent finding a suitable location, on 10 May Alexander and his men built an ingenious crossing. He described it in his diary:

> This is a pontoon or flying bridge, the drays being drawn in a line across the river and the shafts and poles supported by stakes. Long poles are laid from one to the other, on these we have placed hurdles borrowed from [station owner] Mr Brodribb's overseer and, on the hurdles, green boughs. The tarpaulins are laid on the boughs and triced up at the sides to poles fixed to each side of the bridge, forming a hollow or covered way. Some earth is spread all along the bridge. It is strongly moored to a sunken tree.

The bridge was finished the following day and all the sheep crossed within a couple of hours. The Murray River was the next major obstacle on the southward journey and on 14 June Alexander made camp a kilometre from the usual crossing point near present-day Albury. He and his men set about constructing a boat and a punt using materials they had brought with them.

On 17 June the first 300 sheep were carried over the Murray, forty at a time. The next day 800 sheep made the crossing. On the 19th, wrote Alexander:

Ferried over Ashton's flock of sheep and drove the herd of cattle across the river, swimming. All came out of the water but one cow died on the bank. A very strong current carried them 300 yards [275 metres] down the stream before they gained the eddy.

By the 22nd all the sheep were across the river, with the loss of only one lamb, which had been smothered in the punt.

At that stage, Alexander and his stock had been on the road for nearly three months and his patience was wearing thin. On 1 July, he wrote of one of his men:

Since we passed Billabung he [Bryan] has constantly neglected his duty of watching the bullocks at night and our men, with few exceptions, have been growing lazy, careless and insolent, causing much delay and injury.

Alexander didn't seem to make allowances for the fact that during that time his men had endured cold, wet and extremely rough conditions. And it wasn't over yet. Alexander decided he would make camp for a month or so while a thousand of his ewes lambed, and while they were doing so he'd take the opportunity to travel to Melbourne for supplies.

He set out on 12 July with eight men, two drays, twenty-five bullocks and two horses. By the beginning of August they'd made their way down to the new settlement at Port Phillip. The sight of overlanders was still a novelty in the fledgling town. A writer of the time described the picturesque attire many of them wore:

The gentlemen Overlanders affected a banditti style of hair and costume. They rode blood or half-bred Arab horses, wore broad-brimmed sombr-eros trimmed with fur and eagle plumes, scarlet flannel shirts, broad belts filled with pistols, knives and tomahawks, tremendous beards and moustachios … Before the journey became a matter of course, the arrival of a band of these brown, bearded, banditti-looking gentlemen created quite a sensation.

(Samuel Sidney, *The Three Colonies of Australia*)

When it came to choosing a place to camp, the New South Welshmen viewed the Victorian settlers with mistrust. Wrote Alexander:

Charles Bonney, 1859, by S. Solomon. Bonney joined Jospeh Hawdon to take the first cattle overland from the Melbourne district to Adelaide.
(Image courtesy of the City of Norwood, Payneham & St Peters Civic Collection. (State Library of South Australia, B 7390)

The following day, Alexander started loading some of his supplies and storing the remainder. On 4 August he gave his men a day off, ordering them to be ready to set out on the return trip the following morning.

The next day, he lamented his decision: 'My men drunk and unable to come to work.' On the 6th: 'Men drunk and refractory, refusing to come to their duty.' And on the 7th: 'Men still drunk and unable to work or travel. In the afternoon succeeded in getting out of town with the drays. Woods and Collins driving, both drunk.'

It would not be the last instance of stockmen smashing their cheques at the first town they came to after a long trip. Typically, nothing could get Alexander's men back to work until they'd spent every penny of their hard-earned money. Alexander eventually established a station near present-day Malmsbury after a journey that took seven months and one week.

While Alexander had had his fill of overlanding after only one trip, Joseph Hawdon was just getting started. Late in 1837 he began planning his next trip, which he wrote about extensively in his *Journal of a Journey from New South Wales* [which at the time encompassed the Port Phillip district] *to Adelaide*.

His contemporaries thought the journey, over 850 unsettled kilometres, 'rash and Quixotic'. Nevertheless, he rounded up 300 cattle for the expedition from his and his brother John's property at present-day Howlong, near Albury. The men Joseph hired for the expedition were paid twenty shillings per week, double the usual pay for such work. Joseph wrote:

It was amusing to witness the solemnity with which the men signed the Articles. It seemed as if they were signing away their very lives! The distribution of their labours was thus: four of them were to drive the cattle (consisting of 340 head); two to drive the drays, one to have charge of the horses; one to cook, and one to act as my body servant, having the care of my tent and its appurtenances. Each man was armed with a carbine, a pair of pistols, and a bayonet.

Give or take a few men this was the general arrangement of staff in a 'plant', as a droving team and their equipment was called, for overlanding and droving from that time forth. However, most boss drovers didn't have a body servant, while a stockman was usually assigned the job of horsetailer (responsible for finding feed for the horses, having them ready at dawn for work, and looking after the mounts that were being spelled). During difficulties, these roles were abandoned as everyone worked to keep the mob together.

Hawdon was also joined by Charles Bonney, who had just given up trying to raise sheep at a station 60 kilometres north of Melbourne and was keen to investigate the possibilities around Adelaide.

The journey did not start well. On 14 January 1838, Joseph wrote:

One of my men getting blinded with what is termed land blight, I was obliged to send him back to the station. This disease, which appears to be infectious, is very prevalent on the banks of the Hume [as that upper section of the Murray was then known], and frequently continues exceedingly painful for fourteen days. From this accident I was under the necessity of sending only one man forward with the Cattle.

That was just the beginning.

About noon, the heat being most intense, we halted for an hour; but on attempting to proceed the Cattle would not move. The wind began to blow with great violence, and was perfectly hot. Mounting our horses and driving the spare ones before us, we started in search of water. Our kangaroo dogs began howling and could not be induced to follow. Fortunately for me, I was riding my favourite horse, which in twenty minutes carried me six miles [10 kilometres] when I came to a water-hole. Short as the ride was, the heat and violence of the gale made it truly dreadful; it was like riding through a furnace; and so intolerable was my thirst that if I had to go half a mile further, I certainly must have fallen from my horse. In a quarter of an hour from my arrival at the water-hole Mr Weatherall (who started with me from my brother's station on the Hume) came up with the man [suffering land blight], when we made some tea, and rested for a couple of hours. The man went perfectly blind owing, I presume, to the intensity of the heat; we therefore placed him in a hollow tree, the best place of shelter we could find, whilst Mr Weatherall and I rode back to bring up the Cattle. We found them in the position in which they had been left with the exception of one, which, being too fat to bear the heat, had dropped dead.

As people in the bush know only too well, just when you think things can't get worse, they often do. Wrote Joseph:

It was now quite cool, with every appearance of a coming thunderstorm; we had arrived within a quarter of a mile from the water-hole where we

had left the blinded man, when a tremendous peal of thunder burst over our heads. The electric fluid [lightning] passed along my head, causing me to feel as though struck with a heavy bludgeon. Two of the bullocks, within four yards of us, were killed on the spot, one of them standing stiff and dead some seconds before he fell. I exclaimed, 'That beast is standing up after he is dead' but on looking round for Mr Weatherall I saw him supporting his head with his hands. He also had felt the shock, but more severely than myself. A second peal roared and crashed around us, killing another beast about fifteen yards [14 metres] from where I stood. To prevent the whole herd from being killed we galloped among them to scatter them in various directions. One fell struck with the electric fluid whilst I was on the point of striking it. We dismounted for the purpose of bleeding those that had fallen, and while so employed, the tree under which I stood was shivered to pieces. The thunder continued rattling around us, resembling a constant fire of cannon, branches and limbs of trees falling in all directions. We remounted our horses, which stood trembling with terror, that we might better view the surrounding scene. Two hundred of the Cattle had huddled closely together, each trying under an instinctive sense of danger, to screen himself behind his neighbour; the rest, in separate groups of thirty and forty, were flying over the ground in the wildest state of alarm, now running towards us, then bounding away again, as each successive peal of thunder burst.

Miraculously, none of the men were badly injured. Joseph received a small cut. Six cattle were struck by lightning, and three of them died. Undaunted, Joseph and his men continued on their way. Much of the time, Charles Bonney and the men took care of the cattle, while Joseph rode about taking potshots at the wildlife. As he wrote on the 29th:

I returned to the party who, during my absence, had suffered one of the Oxen to get drowned. It appears that being devoured by thirst, the brutes rushed into the river before the men had time to unyoke them, and two of the men had a narrow escape of their lives while trying to disentangle them.

On 11 February, Joseph and Charles reached Swan Hill, which in addition to its namesakes also had an abundance of pelicans, ducks, wild turkeys, parrots and emus. The men also met a large number of Aboriginal people who contested their progress. As the men and cattle advanced, all but one of the Aborigines fell back. Wrote Joseph:

A fine fellow, about six feet [183 centimetres] in height, was actually foaming with eagerness to get his tribe to stand their ground, but on my putting my horse into a gallop to go up the hill to him, he also thought proper to retreat among the reeds, shaking his spear at me as he disappeared.

The overlanders camped in the vicinity that night, and induced the hostile Aborigines to join them. The Europeans made clear their peaceful intentions, and gave a small gift to the warrior who had defied them during the day. As Charles wrote: 'We had no trouble whatever with the natives. At Swan Hill we established friendly relations with them, and from that point until we left the river they always sent forward messengers to the next tribe, to give notice of our approach.' In some areas, the Aborigines they befriended along the way made Joseph and Charles' journey easier. Wrote Charles:

> At last we fell in with three natives, who gave us to understand by signs that they belonged to a tribe lower down the river, and that they would accompany us. One of them I adopted as a guide, and made him understand what I wanted, and such was his intelligent and quick understanding that, though he had never seen a white man before, he seemed to know almost by instinct where a dray could pass and where it could not.

The Aborigine's name was Tenberry, and he was to assist other overlanders through his country as well.

On 19 March Joseph and Charles reached the section of the Murray where it turns south. On the 23rd, the overlanders left the Murray, striking west for Adelaide. Eight days later, wrote Joseph:

> On coming to the seashore we observed the fresh print of a horse's hoof, and following the tract thus obtained, we came upon a tent and hut, in which were residing three young men, who were just commencing a settler's life, their chief occupation at this time was hunting of Kangaroos for the Adelaide market, which they disposed of at a shilling per pound. On my first appearing before them they were at a loss what to make of me; but on my telling them that I had come across the vast wilderness of the interior, they shewed me every possible attention and hospitality.

In a state whose inhabitants were destined to be termed crow-eaters, anyone who arrived with 300 head of cattle was bound to get a friendly welcome. On 4 April Joseph dined with Governor Hindmarsh, 'who expressed himself highly delighted with my arrival, and with the advantages which my arrival with stock would, both immediately, and in its future consequences, entail upon the new Colony.' It would not be the last time that settlers were grateful for the efforts of the Australian stockman. The seeds of a legend had been sown.

Bushmen encamping, lithograph, c.1840, George Hamilton, 1812–1883. An early portrayal of an overlanding or droving 'plant' that included staff, horses and all the supplies necessary for journeys that could extend over months.

(National Library of Australia, an7682877)

Now this is the law of the Overland that
    all in the West obey –
A man must cover with travelling sheep
    a six-mile stage a day;
But this is the law which the drovers
    make, right easily understood,
They travel their stage where the grass is
    bad, but they camp where the grass
    is good.

Banjo Paterson, 'Saltbush Bill'

THE FIRST CATTLE KING

THE LATE HON. JAMES TYSON. One of the most famous
of Australia's squatters. When he died intestate, in 1898,
his estate was valued at between £2,500,000 and
£3,000,000. The above photo. is said to be the only one
he ever had taken.

Poet Will Ogilvie once described the stockman's domain as one in which he had a saddle for a throne. Yet Australia was soon producing stockmen who rose to become kings of all they surveyed. They may have been kings in grass castles, as outback pioneer Patrick 'Patsy' Durack memorably described them – their castles apt to be dispersed on the hot, dry winds of a run of bad seasons – yet they were also potent examples of the rewards that could come from sheer hard work, a good knowledge of stock and a little bit of luck.

Few of the great cattlemen have origins as humble as James Tyson. The man who would become the first 'Cattle King' started life in a rough bush shack at what could be considered the cradle of the Australian beef industry, Cowpastures, on 8 April 1819. He was the seventh of eleven children. His mother, Isabella, was a convict transported for theft in 1809. His father, William, worked his passage aboard the same ship. On their arrival, Isabella was 'assigned' to her husband.

Typical of many bush kids, as soon as James was old enough he went out to work. At age fourteen he was labouring on local properties. In 1837 he got a job working for a bootmaker in Sydney, but the country boy only lasted six months in the city before heading back to the land. As he later recalled, bush life was 'hard work and small wages' but it made a man of him – 188 centimetres tall (just over 6 feet), broad-shouldered and incredibly strong. Soon he was made an overseer, then a station manager, on properties in southern New South Wales.

By the mid-1840s, while still in his mid-twenties, Tyson was looking to strike out on his own. He and his older brother William eventually squatted on land at the junction of the Murrumbidgee and Lachlan rivers. Toorong, on the outer edge of the settled areas of the colony of New South Wales, was so far 'outback' that parts of it hadn't actually been released for settlement by the government. When it was, the Tysons had to buy out the speculator who successfully tendered for the lease. In the meantime they'd flung up basic bush shacks for James, William and his family, and for two other brothers (John and Peter).

By all accounts the early years were extremely hard. Years later, Sidney Kidman, Australia's second cattle king, recalled Tyson's reminiscences of the time: 'He said he was one of the hardest-working men in Australia. He drove a mob of bullocks himself. When they lay down to sleep he slept, and when they woke up he did likewise. He took them over the Blue Mountains to Sydney.'

To make extra money, the Tyson boys also drove stock for other landholders. Stock agent Harry Peck recalled another of Tyson's trips, one that may be more legend than truth:

Rounding up a Straggler, oil on canvas, 1889, Frank Mahony (1862–1916). Returning cattle to a mob was crucial to keeping the mob together. If enough got free, the rest would eventually join them.
(Art Gallery of NSW, 6104)

James Tyson, c.1890. Tyson, also known as Hungry Jim, was Australia's first cattle king. The son of convicts, he built an empire that extended from Queensland to Victoria.
(John Oxley Library, State Library of Queensland, 84-11-20)

He had one shilling to finance the trip, and when he came to the punt at Forbes the river was in flood. The puntman offered to take him across for the shilling when he found that was the extent of the lad's finances, but Jim decided to keep his shilling and swim for it. He did, but nearly lost his life in the crossing. He got the cattle and landed them safely at Juanbung [a later addition to Toorong], a good 500-mile [800-kilometre] journey from there and back, and the shilling still in his pocket. That trip was characteristic of Jim Tyson as a young man, when he denied himself many a necessity in order to save money, and no doubt was the origin of his reputation as a 'possum eater', of which he was not ashamed, for many another good and hardy pioneer had eaten possum and, when properly grilled, relished it, too.

Everything changed for James in 1851. When the existence of gold across New South Wales and Victoria became general knowledge, labourers deserted the countryside and cities became ghost towns as people flocked to the goldfields to make their fortunes. When gold was found at Bendigo, the strike was 300 kilometres from his family's property as the crow flies, 350 by the shortest route that provided sufficient water for stock. That distance presented no difficulties for a family that had been crisscrossing the outback for years. They mustered all the fat cattle they could find and headed for the goldfields.

There James and his brothers did something inspired. Instead of simply selling the cattle to the local butchers and heading back to the farm, they set up their own slaughter yard and butchering business and sold their beef directly to the miners. The idea proved such a goldmine their business became known as Tyson's Reef (referring to a 'reef' or large deposit of the precious metal). Even before they'd run out of their own cattle, the Tyson boys were scouring the surrounding districts and buying cattle from anyone who'd sell. Kidman recalled: 'They bought cattle for about £2, and got £20 a head for them.'

Eventually, the boys were ranging as far away as Queensland, buying stock and droving them back to the goldfields. It took great skill and involved considerable risk to move cattle such long distances – stringing in long lines, down the stock routes, along inland rivers and chains of waterholes, through good seasons and bad – and have them arrive in good enough condition to sell. Nevertheless, by 1855 the highly profitable business had made the whole family a fortune.

It was then that the canny Tysons put the business on the market. It was a bit like selling the goose that laid the golden egg, but the brothers knew enough about gold strikes to understand that sooner or later the gold would run out and the miners would move on. Rather than watch their business slowly decline, they sold at the top of the market.

A lot of people might have retired at that point or gone back to their property to enjoy the comforts of life. Instead, James and John Tyson bought three run-down New South Wales sheep stations – South Deniliquin, Deniliquin and Conargo – all located around the present-day town of Deniliquin. The brothers set about developing the properties with extensive irrigation works, which they could easily fund with their now considerable capital reserves. After the death of his brother John, in 1860, James set about irrigating the original property at Toorong, which had been expanded by the acquisition of adjacent properties to form Tupra-Juanbung, a station that bestrode the Lachlan and Murrumbidgee rivers and extended over more than 200 000 hectares.

Now in his early forties, James was one of the most eligible bachelors in the country. Yet having spent almost all of his life in the bush, he remained single. Stock agent Harry Peck recalled one story that James apparently repeated throughout his life. James described meeting 'one of the finest women he had ever set eyes on' at a wayside shanty perched on a hill in the upper Murrumbidgee, where he was buying cattle for the Bendigo market:

> His description was one of those rare occasions on which he came out of his shell and fairly let himself go. She was his ideal woman, tall, clear-eyed, rosy cheeked, the embodiment of blooming health and constitution. The agents, who had met him for the first time, listened with surprise as they had always thought him to be a 'woman hater'.

James appears to have been genuinely smitten, but like many stockmen, who often outnumbered women in the bush by more than four to one, he may have been too socially inexperienced to begin courting her.

In the place of marriage and family life, James focused his entire attention on his business – acquiring and developing cattle and sheep properties. Key among his acquisitions was the property of Heyfield, in Victoria's Gippsland, in 1865. It was such prime grazing country that he often declared, 'Heyfield can fatten anything.' Now what he needed was a source of cattle needing to be fattened. His eyes turned to Queensland.

In later years poet Banjo Paterson would sing the praises of Queensland's 'sunlit plains extended' but when James started buying land along the Warrego River, on which to breed large numbers of cattle, in the mid-1860s, the plains had plenty of sunshine but not much else. They lacked the vital ingredient – water. However, James had a plan.

Once he'd established himself along the Warrego, he started acquiring holdings further from the river. Next he hired bore contractors and sank wells. Wherever he struck water, he stocked the back blocks. As with his

earlier successes, the idea sounds simple. The big difference was the scale of his plans. In 1868, James held 13 000 hectares along the Warrego. Over the next decade hardly a year went by without him acquiring blocks ranging from 36 000 hectares to 500 000 hectares on the Queensland and New South Wales sides of the border. By 1879 he had created a super-station along the Warrego that covered over a million hectares. It was called Tinnenburra.

The growth of James's empire also gave him a public profile. He was dubbed by newspapers 'The Cattle King', the first time that title had been applied to anyone, let alone the son of a convict mother, born and raised in Australia. However, the convict stain and the disparaging 'possum-eater' reference also remained. As the years passed, James's voracious appetite for land led to *The Bulletin* giving him another title: Hungry Jim. Given his early years of struggle and hardship, it may have been more appropriate than *The Bulletin* intended.

Great wealth doesn't seem to have changed James's way of life. Kidman recalled travelling with him (unlike many absentee landlords he was still riding around his properties even into his seventies) during the strikes of 1891:

> He used to wear a beautiful big gold watch-chain – a bootlace. I do not care what they say about Tyson, I like him. He was a very reserved and humble man. Tyson arrived at Glenormiston Station in Queensland one day, and asked the manager's wife where her husband was. She replied that he would not be back for a day or two, and he said, 'When he returns tell him Tyson is here, and that he is down the creek.' That was nothing unusual for him. I was once at a beautiful place, 40 miles [60 kilometres] from Mount Kosciusko, and the woman there asked me if I had ever met Mr Tyson. She said he had stayed there but had slept outside. There was plenty of hot water at the house, but Tyson said he always washed in the creek as the sand cleaned his hands better than soap.

In his twilight years, when asked about his wealth, Tyson tended to dismiss it with a few words. 'I'm happiest under the stars of heaven, with a bluey for my pillow, and a billy of tea by my side.' James's love of the outback ran deep. In a rare interview he gave *The Brisbane Courier*, he opened his heart. Not for him the nostalgia of Mother England, he was Australian-born and proud of it:

> Our dry, pure, rarefied air, our genial sun, and our boundless space combine to promote the development of animal life in its most vigorous and perfect forms. The rather scanty rainfall, with the almost incessant sunshine, produces sweet and nutritious grasses and herbage such as are found in no other part of the world to my knowledge. Even the physical health of the

animal is conserved as its natural functions are stimulated by the great expanse of country usually in the line of vision. Body and mind are both cultivated through the eye.

In November 1898, approaching his eightieth birthday, Tyson was taken ill at Felton. He refused to see a doctor, saying, 'I have never consulted a doctor in my life and am not going to do so now.' A fortnight later he died in his sleep, his body found on the morning of 4 December.

Tyson's fame ensured a great deal of media comment after his death. Most newspapers referred to him as 'eccentric'. His most vehement critics went much further. *The Bulletin*'s obituary certainly didn't bridle at speaking ill of the recently departed:

> Six foot and a bit he was; but a pretty stunted specimen of humanity all the same, Bulletin reckons. He died so much while he lived that it's no wonder he wouldn't let a doctor try and deprive him of the economy of being dead altogether … In his daily life, and in a small way, Tyson was a mean man – he gave nothing for nothing; but occasionally he could be generous in a large way – that is, as he grew older he gave away considerable sums, and knew himself as rich as he was before … Grit, industry – these were his virtues; and in reclaiming land and breeding stock he helped others, but his chief end was to help himself.

Eventually, his pioneering qualities were recognised. His irrigation projects, vertical integration of his operations and realisation that rail transport was easier on stock than droving were years ahead of their time. His understanding of conditions in the outback, love of the bush and resourcefulness in dealing with its challenges typified the outback spirit. As for his generosity, the shy old bushman tried to keep it hidden but it was not to be. Shortly after Tyson's death, Banjo Paterson, an occasional contributor to *The Bulletin*, wrote a poem, 'T.Y.S.O.N.', for *The Australasian Pastoralists' Review,* that concludes:

> Not by the strait and narrow gate,
> Reserved for wealthy men,
> But through the big gate, opened wide,
> The grizzled figure, eagle-eyed,
> Will travel through – and then
> Old Peter'll say: 'Let's pass him through;
> There's many a thing he used to do,
> Good-hearted things that no one knew;
> That's T.Y.S.O.N.'

1. Tossing for the first pick of a "run."   2. Wild horses leading away the station mares.   3. Stockmen on the march.

SKETCHES   OF

d horses—a kill.   5. Carrying a comrade out of danger.   6. An exploring party trying to win the black fellows to speak with them.   7. The only drop of water for fifty miles round.

STOCKMAN'S   LIFE   IN   AUSTRALIA.

THE
OUTBACK

As stations the size of small countries were established across the Australian outback, a new breed of stockman emerged. The vast emptiness of the interior demanded an unparalleled level of self-sufficiency. In the land of far horizons, where fences were non-existent, stockmen experienced a freedom beyond the comprehension of those who dwelt 'closer in'.

Soon small teams of men and women were herding stock over thousands of kilometres – distances unheard of anywhere else in the world. In addition to their skills in handling stock, they developed leatherworking skills to deal with broken equipment and farriery skills to reshoe their horses. At times they became doctors and performed operations on themselves. Some of the trails they blazed have since become national highways that span the entire continent.

One of the first of the great outback stock routes was the Great North Road. Over the years leading up to 1872, when the Overland Telegraph was built between Adelaide and Darwin, thousands of men were employed along supply lines that extended 3000 kilometres across the country. All those people had to eat, so following in their wake came pioneering stockmen seeking routes for sheep, cattle and horses through country that had defeated explorers only a decade earlier.

One of the longest expeditions, both in distance and time, began even before the Overland Telegraph was thought of. Having heard that the South Australian Government was prepared to pay £2000 to whoever was the first to drive 1000 sheep or 100 cattle overland to Darwin, in 1863 brothers Ralph and John Milner set out with several thousand sheep, intending to follow the explorer John McDouall Stuart's route.

However, soon after they started they became caught in what became known as the Great Drought of the 1860s. The only way to move stock in those times was on the hoof, but soon stock routes were eaten bare and water almost impossible to find. Many cattle perished, dry waterholes littered with the bodies of beasts that had died horribly from thirst and starvation. Such scenes broke the hearts of some stockmen. In some cases, they died with the animals in their care, unable to escape the drought country themselves.

Unable to travel north, the Milners remained in South Australia until 1868, when the drought started to ease. By then, work on the Telegraph had begun, and the hungry construction camps promised to be a ready market for large numbers of stock.

The Milners assembled men, dogs and horses, and headed for the properties run by missionaries at Killalpaninna and Kopperamanna on the Birdsville Track, hoping to acquire more sheep. However, while they were at Killalpaninna events took a tragic turn when Ralph Milner's wife died. She was buried at the station.

Finally, in September 1870, the Milners set out on their trek across Australia. Their equipment included two bullock drays, a horse wagon and two spring carts, twelve months' worth of provisions and material for making pack saddles in case they had to abandon the wagons and drays. Their stock comprised between 4000 and 7000 sheep. The pay for the men was twenty-five shillings a week and a promise of half the government reward shared between them.

Details of the first part of the Milners' journey, which in its entirety was to take more than two years, are few and far between. What is known is that the expedition started at Kopperamanna, headed south past Mundowdna, then turned north-west, following the telegraph line. They spent Christmas Day 1870 at Bulldog Creek, north of Mount Margaret Station, between William Creek and Oodnadatta.

Little is known about their activities in 1871, and the next record doesn't appear until 21 January 1872, when *The Advertiser* reported: 'A telegram from the Government Resident at Port Darwin announces that Mr J. Milner was murdered by natives at Attack Creek.' John Milner had been shepherding the flock at the creek in the Northern Territory, where the explorer Stuart's party had also been involved in a confrontation with Aboriginal warriors in 1860.

The rest of the men succeeded in reaching the Northern Territory's Top End towards the end of 1871. The reward, if it had ever existed, never materialised. As something of a consolation, Ralph Milner managed to sell what remained of his sheep to the Overland Telegraph construction project. However, his difficulties weren't over as the expedition had arrived in the middle of the Top End's wet season. Rivers no longer threaded through the country but had risen and risen until they spread across broad floodplains, turning much of the country into an inland sea, impassable for the stockmen and their sheep.

Nevertheless, the feat of the Milners left a lasting impression on Alfred Giles, a South Australian stockman who had joined the Overland Telegraph construction project as an assistant to John Ross, who established the exact route the line would take. Working for Ross, Giles had already crossed the continent twice. Late in 1872 he was stationed in the Top End at Union Camp, near the junction of the Elsey and Roper rivers.

On 7 December he heard from a party that had come up from the southern construction teams that Ralph Milner was on the Strangways River, with a flock of sheep, a mob of horses and a wagon. Giles wrote in his memoir *Exploring in the Seventies*:

I could scarcely credit a flock of sheep being on the Strangways. Fancy, real mutton not more than 60 miles [100 kilometres] away! These were, un-doubtedly, the first sheep ever brought overland from South Australia, or anywhere else, to the Northern Territory, and Mr. Milner deserved the highest credit for this great pioneering feat.

Ralph Milner wasn't far away but it was two months before his sheep made it to Giles' camp. On 3 February 1872, Ralph arrived on his own, saying he was optimistic that if the weather held, he'd get the sheep through to the Elsey River within a few days.

After Ralph returned to his camp, the Top End was hit by more severe wet weather, with tremendous thunderstorms sweeping across the land. However, Ralph was true to his word. He managed to get the sheep to the Elsey River, where, with the help of some of the telegraph line workers, they succeeded in getting the sheep over the wide, fast-flowing river. Wrote Giles:

> Some of the men carried them over on their backs, as there was no boat where the sheep crossed, which was at a point about three miles [4 kilometres] above the junction of the Elsey and Roper Rivers, whereas the boat or line crossing was 10 miles [16 kilometres] higher up.

By then the sheep had travelled some 2000 kilometres. Alfred Giles cast a bushman's eye over the flock and wrote:

> The sheep, mostly ewes, were small and poor, averaging not more than 30 pounds [13.5 kilograms] dressed weight. I did not attribute their low condition wholly to the distance they had travelled so much as to their being heavily woolled, carrying an 18-months' fleece. The wool was of good quality and staple; the outer, or surface, was frayed and somewhat perished, but considering the unavoidable knocking about the sheep had had, this was not to be wondered at.

While the exact number of sheep Ralph started with isn't clear, he mentioned to Giles that he'd suffered heavy losses during the journey. On one occasion, at the Davenport Ranges south of Tennant Creek, he'd lost 900 head in a single night after they'd eaten a poisonous plant (*Gastrolobium grandiflorum*). A count of the sheep that reached the Top End revealed that from a mob of sheep that may have numbered between 4000 and 7000 when they started out, only 1003 had survived.

Plans were made to distribute the sheep between the various construction parties in the Top End. Alfred Giles volunteered to take 300 head to the camp he was nominally attached to, but which hadn't been heard from for over five months because of the wet. It was thought to be at or near Daly Waters, 250 kilometres south. On 13 February Giles counted out his sheep from the flock and set about getting them shorn, but it was soon apparent that the telegraph men were deficient when it came to shearers. Wrote Giles:

> Shearing in the Northern Territory was a novelty indeed, and among all the Government outfit no such article as sheep-shears was catalogued or thought of. Fortunately, Mr. Milner was able to supply a few pairs. Another remarkable fact was that out of more than 50 men in camp only one knew how to shear, and he happened to be the cook. Under his tutelage, four or five men started shearing, or, perhaps, I should say 'tomahawking'. The main thing was to get the wool off. There was no sorting or preparing. It was just chucked over the fence to rot, and would have grieved the squatter's heart.

The wet season began to show signs of breaking, and by mid-March conditions had improved enough to allow the sheep to be moved. On 11 March Alfred Giles and a colleague, Chris Bagot, rode over to the Elsey River and used a boat to sound the depth to see if the sheep could get across. At a crossing that was more than 200 metres wide, they found that in many places they couldn't touch the bottom with a long pole. They decided there was nothing for it but to boat the sheep over. The problem with that idea was the boat could only carry ten or so sheep at a time, which would mean at least thirty trips.

Alfred rode to another camp and got hold of two coils of wire intended for the telegraph line, then rode back to the river. Securing the wire to a tree on the riverbank, he manoeuvred the boat to a tree in the middle of the stream, secured the wire to the tree, and then tensioned it so it hung about a metre above the fast-flowing river. He then continued to the far bank of the river and secured the end of the wire to another tree. 'By these means,' Giles wrote, 'the boat would be propelled with greater speed, and straighter than with oars.'

On 15 March he and his men brought the 300 sheep to the crossing place. They arrived at 3 p.m. and immediately started the boating operation. Giles soon discovered that he could only get eleven sheep into the boat, and then only if they were packed in tightly. Most ended up in a 'sitting posture – in each others arms, as it were', as if they were out on a nautical excursion. On the first trip, things went awry.

> We had no oars but one man stood in the end of the boat, and, catching hold of the strained wire, pulled the boat along. When half-way across with the first load, the man let go the wire, and in trying to regain it capsized himself, as well as the boat and all the sheep. It was not a strong current, and we

DROVERS IN THE 1870S

The drover fraternity are a distinct feature of the cattle yards gatherings. They are generally rough-looking men, who somehow convey the impression that they seldom wash and never take off their clothes. It is alleged in regard to some of them that their honesty is a little off the centre – that, for instance, if they are so unfortunate as to lose a few cattle on their journeys, they will not scruple to find a few others, if they can, to make up their tally; but they all have the character of proving faithful to their engagements, making it a point of honour to deliver over the stock entrusted to their care at the appointed time, and in as good condition as circumstances will permit.

Australasian Sketcher, 1873

On The Old Man Plain, Riverina – First Scent Of Water – Stockmen Restraining Cattle, wood engraving, 1881, S. Bennett. One of the great challenges with a mob of thirsty cattle is maintaining order when bringing them to water to prevent injuries from stampede or stock drinking themselves to death.
(State Library of Victoria, IAN05/11/81/197)

ON THE OLD MAN PLAIN, RIVERINA.—FIRST SCENT OF WATER—STOCKMEN RESTRAINING CATTLE.

swam in, righted the boat, chased the sheep, and recovered them all, and by dark we had got 124 across. We started to boat again at daybreak the next morning, and got the whole 300 over by 10 o'clock.

Giles and his men battled through the sodden country to Daly Waters, where they found themselves the first new faces to appear in five long, lonely months. Wrote Giles: 'The news that I had 300 sheep within 30 miles [48 kilometres] was most gratifying to the poor fellows, and they actually took off their hats and cheered us.'

Later in 1872 Alfred Giles travelled to the Roper Landing, as the Overland Telegraph work was almost done. The Roper Bar was the landing place for supplies being carried to the construction teams in the interior. During his journey he came upon one of the features that would mark the western starting point of the stock route that would become the Gulf Track:

> We halted for dinner at Mount McMinn, a beautiful and high table-topped mountain close to the Roper River and 12 miles [19 kilometres] from the Roper Landing. On leaving this we passed through a remarkable rocky gorge with immense rocks and twisted stones of every conceivable shape. It has, for some reason, been named Hell's Gates.

The Roper Landing was a bustling depot 120 kilometres up-river from the sea. Most of the men at Roper Landing had been leaving the Northern Territory, never to return. Some, however, were left behind as part of the permanent staff of the completed telegraph line. They included drovers who were responsible for supplying livestock to the telegraph stations dotted along the line, especially in the early days when their vegetable and fruit gardens and herds and flocks of cattle, sheep and goats were being established.

While he was at Roper Landing, Alfred Giles recorded the arrival of the first stock to be overlanded from Queensland:

> On 18th September, 1872, Mr. Dillon Cox arrived with about 400 head of cattle, which, under the charge of his drover, Mr Wentworth d'Arcy Uhr, he had brought across from Queensland. These were undoubtedly the first cattle ever introduced overland into the Northern Territory, and it reflected credit upon Mr. Cox and Mr. Uhr for their plucky enterprise and endurance shown by droving stock across hundreds of miles of perfectly unknown country, risking floods or dry stages, as well as contending with hostile and treacherous savages.

From the scant accounts of the journey, it appears Uhr was a particularly hard man. Following the approximate route taken by explorer Ludwig Leichhardt in 1844–45, he shot any Aboriginal people who dared oppose him. When one of his own men pulled a gun on him, Uhr attacked him with a stockwhip.

The problem for Uhr and Cox was that they'd arrived too late. A big mob of cattle was no longer needed, as the telegraph construction teams were preparing to leave. They were actually slaughtering many of their own bullocks, no longer required for the construction work.

The upshot was that the Roper Landing saw its first court case, to settle a dispute between cattle-owner Cox and stockman Uhr. The case was heard in a mess tent. Cox wanted Uhr to take the cattle on to Darwin, where he had some hope of finding a market for his beef. However, Darwin was several hundred kilometres away and Uhr refused to do the extra work without an additional payment. Eventually a deal was struck and Uhr took the cattle on to what became known as the Cox Peninsula, west of Darwin, where they were slaughtered as required, then boated across and sold to the good citizens of the fledgling town.

Alfred Giles retained his association with the Overland Telegraph. Shortly after its completion, he overlanded 7000 sheep up the Oodnadatta Track, then along the telegraph line and the stock route that serviced it, the Great North Road. In 1874 he was asked to take another 5000 sheep north. In the process of mustering the mob, he met Harris Browne, whose brother W.J. Browne had taken up leases on Springvale and Bonrook Stations, near present-day Katherine. Browne asked Giles to overland stock to the stations in what author Ernestine Hill called 'the greatest cavalcade of droving ever seen in Australia'. Involving 300 horses, 2000 cattle and 12 000 sheep, it was certainly one of the biggest stock movements to the Territory. However, it wasn't the biggest mob that has travelled Australia. Fittingly, that feat fell to the man regarded as the greatest stockman the country has ever seen.

THE GREATEST STOCKMAN

The man many regard as Australia's greatest-ever stockman, Nat Buchanan, was born in Ireland in 1826, the Emerald Isle's forty shades of green as far from the red sandhills and bone-dry gibber plains of the Australian bush as it's possible to get. Even after he arrived in Australia with his parents and four brothers in January 1837, their move to the well-watered pastures of the aptly named New England Plateau of New South Wales was a gentle introduction to the harsh conditions of the Australian bush.

In his twenties, Nat left the family farm and took to the road. He droved (as stockmen put it) cattle to the New South Wales and Victorian goldfields, always hungry to find the opportunity that would set him up on the land. He eventually realised the only option, as James Tyson had found some years earlier, was to go 'run hunting' and head 'further out'.

In 1859, with explorer William Landsborough, he set off from Rockhampton, on the coast of Queensland, to examine inland possibilities for raising stock. The men penetrated to the present-day Thomson River and the site of what would become the town of Aramac, where they found superb downs country that a succession of good seasons had given the appearance of being well watered. Encouraged by what they found, they pressed on until they were running critically low on rations. As the food gave out, they reputedly resorted to eating the greenhide hobbles they'd been using to restrict their horses' movements at night. They put them on to boil when they went to bed at night. By morning the hobbles were reduced to a chewy jelly, not the most appetising breakfast by a long shot, but preferable to the pangs of hunger.

Buchanan returned to central Queensland in 1861 with a land speculator, Edward Cornish, who agreed that the land around Aramac was perfect for sheep. A consortium comprising Landsborough, Cornish, Buchanan and the financiers of the Scottish Australian Investment Company, led by Robert Morehead, took up leases covering almost 3000 square kilometres of what was to become Bowen Downs Station. In 1863 Buchanan was appointed the station's manager. His first job was to drove thousands of sheep from properties in southern Queensland up to the vast new station. He also blazed a new stock route from present-day Bowen, then Port Denison, 483 kilometres inland.

There are few instances of Buchanan having any trouble with the Indigenous inhabitants whose lands he crossed during his early expeditions. It's thought that he had some knowledge of and respect for their customs and tried to be fair in his dealings with them. He also had a habit of telling new men harrowing tales of what had happened to stockmen who'd nodded off during their night watches. Buchanan, meanwhile, slept soundly.

In 1863 Buchanan married Kate Gordon, the daughter of a grazier with properties in northern New South Wales and Queensland. He was sixteen years her senior. Kate had grown up on the land and could ride as well as any man. She was no stranger to the hardships of the bush, but even she must have been daunted by the prospect of following her husband to the isolation of newly established Bowen Downs. When she arrived she was the only white woman on the only property for hundreds of kilometres.

Meanwhile, drought and falling prices saw Bowen Downs fall into debt. In 1866 the price for cattle and wool fell to ruinous levels, and as Nat's son, Gordon, later put it:

> The men who did the pioneering and bore the heat and burden of the day [Landsborough, Cornish and Buchanan] went out without a penny. The sleeping partners, city men, managed to hold on and eventually, as share-holders in one of the most prosperous pastoral holdings in Australia, reaped a rich harvest.

Buchanan returned to smallholdings in New South Wales, while bad seasons plagued central Queensland and the north-west until the mid-1870s. Then Buchanan was offered a job managing Craven Station on the rich volcanic plains near Emerald. The job brought him back to the country of far horizons, a place of unrivalled freedom for those with the skills and resilience to survive and prosper. As the seasons improved he was soon in demand as a drover for mobs of cattle and sheep heading for new pastures in western Queensland.

Once again, the work gave him the opportunity to explore the country farther afield. Buchanan was particularly interested in the country on the Northern Territory side of the border. He may have been accompanied on his journeys by a young Aboriginal man from the Gulf, known only as Jimmy. The two men reputedly could match each other for endurance, especially when it came to going without water. Throughout his life, when other Europeans were desperately thirsty, Buchanan could get by with just a mouthful. He could also make do with rations that were well past their use-by date. He was once observed sieving weevils out of his flour. When it was suggested the flour was rotten, he simply replied that it couldn't be too bad if the weevils were still eating it.

Buchanan's explorations led him to pioneer a route across the Barkly Tableland (with fellow stockman Sam Croker), a journey that revealed many of the water sources on that incredibly rich expanse of open grassland.

At the beginning of 1878 he was asked to take 1200 cattle from Aramac Station, near Bowen Downs in central Queensland, to Glencoe Station, just south of present-day Darwin. It was a journey of 2250 kilometres, 1600 of them through trackless wilderness. No one had attempted anything like

it before. The explorer Leichhardt had pioneered the route on one of his expeditions in the 1840s. Only two small mobs of cattle and one mob of horses had previously attempted the Gulf Track, as it was to become known.

Buchanan quickly established the daily routine. Every morning he set off ahead of the drovers and passed the site he'd selected the day before for that night's camp (while leaving clear tracks for the stockmen to follow). He then started scouting for the following night's campsite. Every day he rode between 30 and 50 kilometres, before returning around nightfall to the new camp.

Although the daily distances were kept short for the sake of the cattle, there was still plenty of work for the stockmen. An hour before daylight the horsetailer started rounding up the horses that were to be used for that day's work (horses usually worked one day on and two off). The cook had breakfast ready before dawn. At first light, as the sun extended its first tentative rays over the eastern horizon, the cattle were roused with a cracking of stockwhips and the shouts of the stockmen. During the morning the horse drover and cook overtook the cattle with the drays and spare horses, hastening forward to set up that night's camp. The stockmen usually carried their lunches with them. In Buchanan's case it consisted of nothing more than a pocketful of dried raisins. Dinner at the night camp usually comprised 'bully' beef (tinned corned beef so named because it originally came from Booyoolee Station and was initially called Booyoolee beef), damper, potatoes, rice and dried apples. Occasionally there was fresh beef when one of the cattle was killed or died as a result of an accident.

After dinner a night watch was set around the cattle to ensure they didn't stray or, worse, stampede from fear or confusion. Each stockman's watch usually lasted two or three hours. Two men were assigned if the cattle seemed restless or Aboriginal people were in the vicinity, which was often the case. The average working day was fifteen or sixteen hours, seven days a week. The men were given a couple of hours off per week to wash their clothes.

Just over the Northern Territory border, at Redbank Creek, the camp experienced its first Aboriginal attack, when one of the horses was speared and killed during the night. Sixty kilometres further on, another horse was speared, prompting Buchanan to set a watch on the horses as well as the cattle. During the day, on the Calvert River, Aboriginal warriors threatened the stockmen from the high stone cliffs carved by the river when it rose in the turbulence of a wet-season flood.

Beyond the Calvert the Aborigines finally left the drovers in peace, but at the Robinson River, which the drovers reached where it was tidal, another menace reared its head – saltwater crocodiles (*Crocodylus porosus*). The giant reptiles may not have seen cattle before, but they pounced on this new kind of prey as soon as the stock came near the water, mauling several.

At the Macarthur River, supplies were starting to run low. Nat decided to ride with Wattie Gordon to the Katherine Telegraph Station, 500 kilometres away, to secure extra rations. Free from the slow-moving cattle, Buchanan and Gordon covered the distance to Katherine in less than a week.

While he was away the Aborigines at the Limmen River attacked the stock camp. The nephew of one of the stock owners, W. Travers, was on his own, making damper. He had a loaded revolver in his belt but he never got a chance to use it. When the other men returned to the camp they found him dead, almost decapitated by a blow from an axe, his hands still covered in dough. It wasn't clear if he'd allowed someone into the camp or been surprised by a sudden attack. Everything had been ransacked and most of the remaining supplies were gone.

Despite his desire to maintain good relations with the Aborigines, on his return Buchanan allowed a punitive expedition to be mounted. Then the cattle were mustered in preparation for moving on, whereupon it was found that up to twenty-five had been speared. Rather than become embroiled in a cycle of tit for tat, Buchanan decided not to engage in further reprisals. The stock was soon at the Wickham River, where a short stretch of dense scrub made life difficult for the cattle and the drays. Once through, Buchanan set a course across country, heading east to the Hodgson River, a tributary of the Roper. He then travelled down through the rocky gorge of what became known as Hell's Gates. After that, the worst was behind them.

By then, Glencoe had been sold to new owners. In July 1881 they asked Buchanan to stock both Glencoe and a smaller station on the Daly River with another mob of cattle. Of course he'd done it all before, but this time there was one major difference. The owners, Lyons and Fisher, wanted him to move 20000 head. This was by far the biggest mob of cattle ever droved in Australia.

The question of where to get 20000 head of cattle was resolved by Lyons and Fisher, who owned several stations in southern Queensland, near the town of St George. Huge cutting-out camps were established on the stations. Great clouds of dust rose over the sunlit plains as thousands of cattle were mustered. As the drafts of cattle for the road were being assembled and branded, the growing mobs were held on camp by stockmen who circled them night and day. For many, a hard day of mustering was followed by a night watch, with up to four more hours in the saddle. Under the circumstances, it wasn't hard to rack up sixteen hours a day on horseback. When they weren't working, the men slept – anytime, anywhere. It was a taste of things to come.

Drovers Cutting Cattle from the Herd, print, 1882. The skills of Queensland stockmen were tested at this time when Nat Buchanan took 20 000 Queensland cattle overland to the Top End of the Northern Territory.

(John Oxley Library, State Library of Queensland, 55749)

In a biography of his father, Gordon Buchanan (aged seventeen at the time) recalled:

> The cutting-out camps were centres of furious activity and apparent confusion. Sweating horses and men were inextricably linked with the ever-circling herd, amid the dust. But it was not so. The confined body of cattle with two horsemen, cutters out, riding through them, was very difficult to keep together. It required from six to ten men continually riding around the circumscribed area of the cutting out camp to prevent spreading and occasional breakaways from the bellowing, insurgent and rebellious throng.
>
> The good camp horse knows his quarry as soon as the whip or spur is popped on him and is the embodiment of speed, dexterity, intelligence and beauty. Propping, jumping, wheeling on his hind legs, anticipating by a fraction of a second every refractory turn of a beast. All his rider has to do is sit on him – not an easy job for some, but an intensely exhilarating one. He is the complete artist and is reserved almost entirely for this work.
>
> (Buchanan, G., *Packhorse and Waterhole*, Angus & Robertson, Sydney, 1933)

When the cattle started their journey, the stockmen from the stations who'd helped with the mustering stayed with each mob for a couple of days to help the drovers train them for the new routine of travelling.

Having seen them on their way, Nat and a lively young stockman called Tom Cahill headed to Woodhouse Station near Townsville to buy horses. Some 500 were destined for the Glencoe and Daly River stations, while others were needed for the sixty or so men droving the mobs. When they had 120 unbroken horses, Tom, his brother Matt and an unnamed Aboriginal stockman drove them west towards Richmond Downs Station on the Flinders River, near the present-day town of Richmond.

Tom was not much bigger than a jockey but he had more than his share of skill and courage. His strategy for managing the untrained horses was to keep them tired and hungry. In the morning, with Tom in the lead and Matt and the Aboriginal stockman pushing the mob along from the rear, they trotted the horses along the road. They were given a spell of rest at midday. Then they pushed on to night camp, covering up to 50 kilometres in a day. At night, the tired horses were less inclined to stray far from camp while they grazed.

As they travelled, the three young men took advantage of any yards they came across to pause for a day or two to break in some of the horses. Some stockmen believe that breaking in on the road has the advantage that the horses end up being quieter and easier to catch, plus they learn their lessons better when they go straight from being broken in to working with cattle.

A demon to handle! A devil to ride!
Small wonder the surcingle burst;
You'd have thought that he'd buck himself out of his hide
On the morning we saddled him first.
I can mind how he cow-kicked the spur on my boot,
And though that's long ago, still I vow
If they're wheeling a piker no new-chum galoot
Is a-riding old Harlequin now!

Harry 'Breaker' Morant, 'Who's Riding Old Harlequin Now?'

The furiously busy Nat Buchanan had already organised the purchase of another 4500 cattle from Richmond Downs, and by the time he arrived at the station most of the mob had been mustered. Unfortunately, the entire mob rushed one night and flattened a large part of the fencing where they'd been yarded. The mustering had to start over, and with the yards destroyed the mob had to be watched night and day by circling stockmen.

The delays and rushes cost one stockman, Paddy Fitzpatrick, his life. He had galloped his horse to the head of a rush of 1200 cattle and was trying to turn the leaders, when his horse fell. The rushing cattle ran right over Fitzpatrick and he was trampled to death.

Eventually all the mobs were on the road, rivers of cattle converging at the remote outpost of Burketown. There, many of the men went on strike for better wages. A handful of loyal stockmen and drovers were left to tend the immense herd.

The situation was dire, but as time went on, men gradually made their way back to the stock camp. In time-honoured tradition, they'd handed all their money over the bar. Now most were broke. As the cattle started to move, they didn't want to be left behind with neither job nor money.

The lead mobs were 80 kilometres west of the Northern Territory–Queensland border when half a dozen Aboriginal men approached Tom Cahill's team. The area around the Calvert River was regarded as a place where the Indigenous population was particularly threatening. The passage between the sea and the escarpment narrowed to such an extent that spears could be thrown almost with impunity at unsuspecting men and beasts below.

In contrast to their fearsome reputation, the men who faced Tom Cahill appeared to be friendly. Tom's men had just killed a beast, and in an attempt to foster good relations he gave the Aboriginal men all the meat and bones they could carry.

There was another encounter the following day. A single Aboriginal man, in ceremonial paint and headdress, waded across the river and called on Tom's camp. He may have been trying to negotiate for more beef but the discussions were soon interrupted. Wrote Gordon Buchanan:

> No unfriendliness was shown him, nor did he appear at all alarmed until the Malay horse-hunter, who was wearing a white hat (and excepting that and his colour in no way differing from the other drovers) appeared in the distance. When the Malay, who was on horseback, was nearing the camp, the blackfellow jumped up, gave him one look of horror and alarm, and ran for his life, disappearing over the riverbank as if seven devils were after him.
>
> No explanation of this terror was ever forthcoming. He may have imagined something supernatural in the Malay's appearance. On the other hand, the memory of some depredation by the Malays, who used to visit the northern coasts of Australia, may have filled him with fear. However, there was no further intercourse, friendly or unfriendly, with those blacks after that.

At the Wearyan River, one of the stockmen, W. Sayle, fell ill and died. The nature of his illness was never diagnosed. His body was buried on the track, another addition to the unknown number of lonely graves scattered throughout the outback, many of which have long since disappeared. Where a simple wooden cross was used, termites devoured any evidence. In places, a pile or ring of stones remains. In a few instances, iron surrounds and head-stones can be seen, erected by grieving relatives long after their son, brother, husband or father had perished, far from hearth and home.

> And oft in the shades of the twilight,
> When the soft winds are whispering low,
> And the darkening shadows are falling,
> Sometimes think of the stockman below.
>
> Anon, 'The Dying Stockman'

It wasn't all danger and tension. The long line of cattle (which, broken into smaller mobs, stretched for over 90 kilometres) averaged a distance of

between 10 and 15 kilometres a day, and in places the country opened out to grasslands studded with woollybutt and ironbarks. The cattle were now trained to the road, and many had their preferred positions in the slowly grazing mobs. Day after day passed without incident but Gordon Buchanan maintained that droving the mobs was anything but boring:

> Besides [the stockman's] interest in the cattle, many of which were individually known and would at once be missed if not in the mob, the flora and bird and animal life often claimed his attention.
>
> The venomous green tree ant, which builds its nest in the gathered leaves of the branch end, and the rifle fish, which shoots insects by squirting a jet of water at them, together with the corkscrew or pandanus palm, which lines the permanent watercourses, the feather palm, green plum tree, etc., all came under his observant eye.
>
> And in the bright starry nights with occasional meteors, on the morning watch when the cattle were usually quiet, the heavens with their wonder and mystery would lead his thoughts to the Great Creator of all. The Great Comet [visible from September 1882 until February 1883] of that year was also an absorbing interest in the early morning.

On 16 December 1882, the *The Northern Territory Times & Gazette* noted a telegram it had received from the manager of Elsey Station on 11 December: 'Warby passed Elsey yesterday with 1616 head of cattle. Also a mob of Buchanan's cattle. Both mobs for Glencoe.'

Buchanan's mob may have been the one with Tom Cahill in charge, as he and Warby arrived at the Katherine River crossing at almost the same time. Warby got to the river ahead of Tom Cahill, but only just. He was keen to keep his lead over the youngster and, throwing caution to the wind, drove his mob straight into the fast-flowing water. His stockmen were on hand to guide the mob across. However, when the lead cattle got into the middle of the river and started swimming, they panicked and tried to turn back. The weight of the mob behind kept pressing forward and now the river turned into a white foam of more than 1600 colliding, thrashing beasts. The current swept them downstream as chaos reigned. Seventy cattle drowned, as did one of the stockmen's horses, forcing the stockman to swim for his life. A few cattle made it to the far side, but most ended up back on the southern bank, a kilometre downstream, where it took Warby a day to round them up.

Tom was wiser in the ways of stock. When he arrived at the crossing, he began by swimming a few of the leading cattle across to the far side of the river before sending the bulk of the mob into the water. The main body of cattle could see their mates on the far side, the ones who tended to lead the mob anyway, and swam towards them. The whole mob emerged from the river on the far side without incident.

The rivalry between Tom and Warby continued for all of the remaining 120 kilometres to the stockyards at Glencoe. There the station manager insisted on counting the cattle as they were yarded. Wrote Gordon:

> Cahill's cattle were the nearer, but Warby met him between the wings as [Tom] was opening the big double gates, and with blustering challenge claimed priority.
>
> 'My lot is going through first, Tom. Get out of the way.'
>
> But Tommy, five feet two [157 centimetres] in his socks, stood his ground. His burly rival threatened to knock him down.
>
> Tommy's blue eyes flashed as he picked up a stout but supple yarding stick.
>
> 'Come another step closer, Warby, you bloody big bully and I'll lay you out. If this won't stop you, I have something here that will!' putting his hand on his revolver. Warby's was on his saddle some hundred yards away. Bluff or not, that staggered Warby.
>
> 'Go on then, yard 'em up you cantankerous little fat bastard.'

With the money he was earning droving other people's cattle, Buchanan could finally afford to take up leases on the country he'd explored west of the Overland Telegraph line. Even as he was delivering the cattle to Glencoe, he had a mob of his own cattle on the Gulf Track bound for a property he was forming with his brothers-in-law – Wave Hill, in the Victoria River District. Once again he blazed the trail to the property, in the process helping stock one of the largest properties in the world, Fisher and Lyons' newly acquired Victoria River Downs. From there he took 4000 head to the Ord River, in Western Australia, pioneering a 450-kilometre direct route from Katherine. Just as he'd crossed Queensland via a mixture of stock routes and exploring trips, he'd now crossed the Northern Territory (and nearly two-thirds of Australia). He had also helped establish two of Australia's iconic stations: Bowen Downs and Wave Hill. It was an epic achievement but he wasn't finished yet.

Wave Hill was to be Buchanan's base of operations for more than a decade, despite being extremely remote. Buchanan's search for markets eventually led him to pioneer two more stock routes. One, the famous Murranji, provided a shortcut to eastern markets, which were still several thousand kilometres away. The other crossed to the Western Australian coast and headed south towards Perth. Although the route was seldom used, it still meant Nat had pioneered stock routes that extended from one side of Australia to the other, an achievement unrivalled among stockmen.

Floods in the Interior, Shifting Cattle to High Ground, wood engraving, 1883. Throughout Australia's history, floods have caused massive stock losses, while stockmen have gone to extraordinary lengths to save as many animals as they can.

(State Library of Victoria, AN05/09/83/145)

It was to no avail. Eventually, his brother William, who had underwritten much of the expense of Wave Hill, bought out Nat's share, leaving Nat with nothing, as his share from the sale didn't cover his share of the debts on the property.

Despite the succession of disappointments he'd endured trying to gain his own foothold on the land, Buchanan still enjoyed legendary status across the north of Australia. Many of the stations and districts that were now successfully raising cattle owed their genesis to him. In 1896 the *Northern Territory Times & Gazette* described him thus:

> [He is] an unassuming explorer who has a far better claim to renown than most of the crowd who have posed of later years as Australian explorers. He must be now seventy years of age and he is possibly too old to stand many severe bush crises, but in his best day nothing was too rough for him . . . Hundreds of bush yarns are current about 'Old Bluey', as stockmen familiarly call him, but in none of them have we ever traced anything but the most flattering recognition of the good work done by Buchanan in the pioneering days of the Far North.

He was also known among Aboriginal people as Paraway, a corruption of his answer 'Far away' to their questions about where he was going next. It's perhaps fitting that his respect for Aboriginal people, demonstrated particularly in his relations with the inhabitants of Wave Hill, ensured that they were still on their country, working as stockmen, when in the 1960s Wave Hill became the flashpoint that led to the Aboriginal land rights movement.

In 1899 Buchanan's health started to fail him. He and Kate finally left the Kimberley and moved back to the milder climate of New South Wales. He bought Kenmuir, 10 hectares of land near Tamworth, where he grew lucerne to help make ends meet. It was a humble ending for a man *The Bulletin* described as having helped settle more new country than any other man in Australia. His legacy spanned the continent. The greatest stockman the outback has ever known died on 23 September 1901.

Two young stockmen shoeing one of their horses in the blacksmith's shop on 'Bluff Downs', North Queensland, 1961. The leather bellows being used is believed to have been carted in by bullock cart during the early development days of the station, in the late 1800s.
(W. Brindle, National Archives of Australia, A1200, L39313)

A TEST OF LOYALTY

For stockmen out on Victoria River Downs, the remote location meant that supplies were often delayed. In November 1926, the plight of the station's manager, Alf Martin, was documented in newspapers around the country after he gave an interview in Darwin.

The station was paralysed because supplies of food and clothing hadn't arrived. Local Indigenous people who worked as stockmen had 'gone bush' to find food. The white stockmen had been living on nothing but beef and damper for the whole year. Alf's wife and seven children were also on basic rations.

In October Alf had gone to the landing on the Victoria River where his carrier, with thirteen bags of flour and some petrol, was waiting for a coastal steamer to arrive from Darwin. He'd been waiting since April. Alf then went to Katherine and bought supplies of what he could, then paid for it to be carted to the station at a cost of £22 10 shillings a ton; the total cost of flour at the station was more than £42 a ton.

According to the reports: 'The only thing which had saved this vast property from being abandoned was the loyal conduct of the men employed, who had lived on miserable rations for months past; but, knowing that the station owner had made every possible endeavour, loyally stuck to their post.'

View Of Mummell, An Estate Near Goulburn, NSW, wood engraving, 1857, Walter G. Mason. Cattle dogs are being used here as the southern regions of Australia having 'softer' ground that causes less damage to their paws than the northern regions.
(National Library of Australia, an808804)

THE DEAD HEART

The Queenslander

ILLUSTRATED WEEKLY

6d

POSTAGE: Commonwealth, N.Z., New Guinea, Mandated Territories, and Fiji, 2d.; Britain and Ireland, 2d. (all sea route, 2d.); other parts of the British Empire, 2d.; U.S.A. and Foreign Countries, 4d.

May 10, 1934.

The Big Boss Cattle Drover

It was perhaps inevitable that the stock route that passed through the region of south-west Queensland known as Heartbreak Corner would become one of the most famous in the country. The 650-kilometre Birdsville Track extends from the red sandhill and gibber-rock country of Queensland's Simpson Desert down to the railhead at Marree, in South Australia. While the track follows the rivers of the Channel Country towards Lake Eyre, which bring forth an explosion of nutritious fodder when they flood, it can also be one of the hottest, driest and unforgiving places on Earth. And it has bred some of the most legendary stockmen of the outback.

Given the cool winters and ferociously hot summers, droving down the Birdsville Track quickly became seasonal. From mid-autumn to mid-spring, a period of six months, the daytime temperatures usually only reach the twenties. Overnight, the temperature can fall to freezing. If water and feed is about, it won't dry out and blow away in the cool conditions.

According to explorer Cecil Madigan:

The present system is for cattle to be bred in the Gulf Country and Northern Territory, from whose stations they are brought down on the hoof, to be fattened in the Channel Country. Several pastoral companies own breeding and fattening properties in these areas, running them in conjunction; others buy stores to fatten in the south ... A mob of stores may take four or five months to travel from the Barkly Tableland to the Diamantina. By that time not only has the flood subsided, but the top-feed has dried off. On the other hand, if there is no flood, pastoralists dare not bring down big mobs, which might well perish.

Birdsville, the town that gave the stock route its name, was (and still is) a frontier town. The customers the town's three pubs served might have been rough and ready, but the publicans could give them a run for their money, in every sense. Stockmen, many of them illiterate, would pass their pay cheques over the bar and tell the publican to stop serving them when the money ran out. Soon they were too drunk to know how much they'd drunk, let alone what it had cost them. The arrangement seldom gave value for money.

Oh, so I must be going, I've a mighty way to go,
Till I drink artesian water from a thousand feet below,
And meet the overlanders with their cattle coming down,
We'll work a while, and make a pile, and have a spree in town.

Anon, 'A Bushman's Song'

Previous spread:
Stockmen and cattle from 'Marion Downs' on Beefwood Sandhill on the Birdsville Track, 1930. Stations on the western rivers of Queensland took cattle down the track to South Australia in the cooler times of the year when there was sufficient feed available. It could be a lonely challenging trip through the 'big sky' country of what has been described as Australia's 'dead heart'.
(E. L. Walpole, State Library of South Australia, B 47089/166)

Illustrated front cover from *The Queenslander*, 1934, James Wieneke (1906–1981). When compared to the image of Harry Zigenbine on page ix, Wieneke's presentation of a drover of the time appears to be accurate.
(John Oxley Library, State Library of Queensland, 702692-19340510-s001b)

Stockmen on motorbikes and in utilities muster cleanskins in the dunes near Crown Point Station, in the so-called Dead Heart of Australia, 2011.

(Evan McHugh)

Another practice in the Channel Country townships of Urandangi, Dajarra, Boulia, Bedourie and Birdsville was the use of what was called a shin plaster. These were I.O.U.s signed by publicans and storekeepers in lieu of actual money, given in change when a cheque wasn't completely spent. They were about the size of a large sticking plaster, hence the name. Some bush publicans baked their shin plasters so they would disintegrate soon after they were given out.

Not all stockmen were taken in by the practices of the pubs. One Aboriginal stockman reputedly asked his boss if he could be paid with two cheques: 'One big fella, one little fella.' He gave the smaller cheque to the publican, and found that it made little difference to how long the grog lasted.

A bullock drover had a more unorthodox approach to getting value for money. At a pub in the Boulia region, he woke after a big night to be told that his cheque had cut out. As he prepared to leave, he asked for a bottle of rum, the usual gift after a customer had spent a large sum in the bar. The publican refused. So the drover hitched his bullock team to the pub's veranda posts and threatened to tear the place down. The publican hurried out with three bottles of rum, a small price to pay to save his establishment.

Over time, bores were sunk along the Birdsville Track to provide water for the mobs of travelling cattle. However, there was still plenty of potential for things to go wrong. Around 1899, in the midst of drought, drover Jack Clarke got caught out.

Clarke had picked up 500 bullocks from an Elder Smith property, Warenda, north-east of Boulia, with instructions to deliver them to Sidney Kidman in Birdsville. Clarke droved the stock down the Georgina, past Kidman's Glenglye and Carcoory stations, to Birdsville.

Kidman's agent wasn't there. There was a letter telling Clarke to push on to Andrewilla Waterhole, where a Kidman drover would meet him. Clarke carried on through country that had been withered by drought for at least three years. There was virtually nothing for the cattle to feed on but he managed to reach Andrewilla, a long and deep sheet of permanent water 75 kilometres south of Birdsville, on the South Australia side of the border. When he got there, there was no Kidman drover. Instead, there was a South Australian customs officer demanding border duties of £1000, which, not surprisingly, Clarke didn't have. Eventually a letter arrived from Kidman saying he wasn't going to take delivery of the cattle unless they were brought down to Marree. Clarke decided to press on. He had just struggled over 650-odd kilometres of dry country, and whatever there was in the 500 kilometres ahead couldn't be worse than what lay behind.

Clarke sent a stockman forward to scout for water. Goyder Lagoon turned out to be dry as a wood chip. The Round Hole, which was considered to be

permanent water, was empty. At Potato Tin Sandhill there was just enough water for the stock to get a drink. Clarke moved the stock down then set out for the bore at Mungerannie. He got there without mishap and gave the stock a break.

Clarke may have been travelling the stock during the droving season, but considering the cattle were being taken from a Channel Country station it may have been closer to summer. In any case, Clarke decided to get the cattle moving at midnight on the long dry stage to Kopperamanna Bore, 80 kilometres south. At nine the following morning, Clarke's luck ran out.

A red-grey cloud appeared on the horizon, rapidly growing as it advanced towards them. Soon it was filling most of the sky and the cattle became unsettled, threatening to run. The stockmen moved to steady the mob before they rushed. They managed to hold them in a bunch as the cloud grew.

Jack Clarke asked another stockman, 'Reckon that's rain or dust?'

'I think it's rain,' he replied.

'If it is, we're blessed,' Jack said. 'If it's dust, we're cursed.'

A cool breeze sprang up, suggesting the cloud might be bringing rain. The bullocks thought so, too, and had their heads up, sniffing the air hopefully. Then came the realisation that the cloud reached to the ground and was actually columns of dust stretching far into the sky.

When it hit, day turned to night, calm to screaming wind, and blinding, choking dust swirled around the men, their horses and the cattle. No one could face the onslaught, instinctively turning away from it and huddling together for protection. The dust was so thick the men couldn't see their hands in front of their faces.

Some dust storms herald a passing front and are over quickly. As the hours wore on through the morning and into the afternoon, there was no sign of this one breaking. The men hobbled their horses, unsaddled and unpacked them. They dropped the packs in the dust, which soon buried them. Some of the pack saddles were never found again.

Night was approaching when the storm eased a little. Man and beast had endured a terrible day but Jack knew he had to get his thirsty cattle moving. When the men tried to get the bullocks to rise, they found seventy had been smothered by dust where they lay.

The suffering, disoriented cattle were in no mood to move. Some attacked others that were in their death throes. Jack described them as having eyes 'like balls of fire in the dust'. Eventually, they got the survivors walking but then the dust storm regained its intensity. The mob circled back in on itself, with men and horses seeking shelter as well.

It was impossible to go further. The mob and the men gathered in a bunch again and stayed in a tight group throughout the night. Towards morning, some of the remaining 430 bullocks tried to rush. The stockmen lost more than thirty, but managed to hold most of the mob together.

As the sun rose, the storm finally relented. However, it had been impossible to travel the stock far during the night, and they were still 27 kilometres from water. They had to get a drink but as the sun rose the day grew terribly hot. As the stockmen pushed the mob onwards, bunches of them collapsed and died along the way. Yet the stockmen knew that if they didn't keep going, all of them would go the same way. The dreadful march went on for kilometre after kilometre. At last they reached Cooper Creek with just seventy-five head from the original mob of 500.

After refreshing himself and his horse, Jack Clarke went back to track the cattle that had rushed. Some had reached Cooper Creek 16 kilometres from the main mob. Jack found them on a claypan, walking in single file, 'slowly, lost, half-blinded, heads hanging'.

He found another thirty head at a waterhole that had become salty as it had evaporated. Only two were still alive. The other twenty-eight had drunk and drunk the salty water until it killed them. More cattle died before the mob was able to travel beyond the Cooper. Eventually, Jack was able to save only seventy-two head out of 500.

On all the earth there is no sadder sound
Than moan of cattle when their thirst is great;
It quivers in the trees, and sky and ground
With all its hopelessness reverberate:
This heart-cry of the dumb brutes in the wild
That sears you like the sobbing of a child.

Will Ogilvie, 'The Overlander'

Such disasters may have emphasised the perils of the Birdsville Track, but they didn't discourage drovers from using it, especially in a good season. Cecil Madigan noted that when he was at Birdsville, in the late 1930s, six mobs of cattle were within one or two days' travel from the town. Madigan and some of his colleagues travelled down the track, making scientific observations along the way. Madigan also witnessed aspects of life for stockmen in that era. He wrote in his book, *Crossing the Dead Heart*: 'When I asked one drover about his difficulties he made a very wise remark that applies to leaders in all walks of life, and I have often quoted it since. He said a drover must know more than his men and do more than his men.'

Stockmen in western Queensland still speak in awed tones of 'Mulligan Bulls', wild cattle from the Simpson Desert country beyond the Mulligan River, the most westerly river in the state. Here they're trying to brand one using a fork attached to a tree and a rope tethered to a horse (out of picture) to pull it up. With a fore and hind leg roped, the beast will be dropped on its side, immobilised. The likelihood of injury (to stock and stockmen) during such an exercise was high. This technique is kept alive in the sport of bronco branding.
(State Library of South Australia, PRG280/1/36/219)

It was another good year in the late 1940s when George Farwell, author of *Land of Mirage*, travelled down the Birdsville Track. Cattle were coming down in an endless stream once again. Drover Ted Sheean told Farwell that he reckoned 30000 had travelled the track south over the six months of the droving season and eaten the country bare.

On his trip Farwell met another of the many great characters of the Birdsville Track, Bill Gwydir. Bill was renowned as a stockman and drover, and was more at home on a horse than on his own two feet. He'd been droving since the age of fifteen, when he'd started out as a horsetailer.

At eighteen, Gwydir became a boss drover. He took a mob of store cattle from Marion Downs to New South Wales, where they gave him a bonus for delivering the stock in particularly good condition. He then worked as head stockman on Glenglye. He took a job in Sydney for a while, working in the Homebush cattle saleyards, but he didn't last long.

'City life,' he'd said, 'that's enough to kill a man. By hell, I went for my life back to the mulga. Out here a man's free as a frog from feathers.'

Farwell regarded Gwydir's accent as typical of the region: 'The leisurely, far-riding life of the cattle country, with its adventurous spirit and cyclic bursts of energy, gains its expression in something I like to term the "Queensland voice". It is a rugged, half-bantering, superbly confident voice, carrying an echo of ballad poetry and an Irish brogue.'

It can still be heard in western Queensland today. Stockmen young and old, Aboriginal and European, will meet strangers with a confident, 'How's it goin'?' Driving in an unhurried manner borrows the droving term 'poking along'. Babysitting is referred to as 'tailing the kids'. Even sitting in a room waiting to see the Flying Doctor is referred to as being 'yarded up'.

When Farwell met Bill Gwydir, he was riding a stocky grey horse, with fetlocks so large he looked to be a young draught horse. Such horses were used to 'bronco brand' cattle, the traditional method of roping cattle and using the horse to pull them up to a timber branding panel where they were tipped on their side before being branded.

When Gwydir dismounted, his spurs clinked on the red gibber rocks strewn across the ground. He wore a leather coat, leather leggings and tight-fitting pants, a broad-brimmed hat much stained, weathered and holed, trimmed with a feather from a black cockatoo. A pair of dust goggles completed his outfit.

One of Bill's renowned exploits was bringing 600 head of cattle from the western side of the Simpson Desert to Mungerannie Station on the Birdsville Track, at the beginning of the drought of 1945. The feat hadn't been attempted since the turn of the century.

The cattle belonged to another of the famous figures of the Birdsville

Track, Jim Oldfield, whose family can still be found running stations in central Australia to this day. Jim was to meet Bill 80 kilometres east of Macumba Station with fresh horses, and they'd bring the stock through together.

However, most old hands were sceptical. 'You'll perish the cattle and you'll perish your men,' was the general verdict. They reckoned the lower Diamantina was all undrinkable salt water, the result of the waterholes evaporating.

While Jim scouted out waterholes along the Kallakoopah through to Lake Eyre, then tracked up the main, almost bone-dry channel of the Macumba, which in places spreads out to become 40 or 50 kilometres wide, Bill was droving the cattle down the Macumba, but finding precious little feed to keep them going.

When Jim finally found him, Bill was out of supplies and his horses were thin and exhausted. From what Jim had seen of the country he'd scouted, turning back now seemed a good idea. But Bill had made it this far, and with Jim's fresh horses, he wasn't about to quit. The pair finally agreed to keep going.

A flood had come down the Macumba some months before, which meant there was still water about, although it was brackish. Summer was approaching, which didn't help matters. Nevertheless, all went well until they reached the Kallakoopah. There they managed to bog a dozen bullocks while trying to get them to water. The men had to go into the water up to their waists to try to get them out.

When they ran short of supplies, Jim Oldfield rode ahead to Cowarie Station to get more. At that point Jim hadn't been heard from for weeks, and Bill Gwydir hadn't been heard from for even longer. The general opinion had been formed that all the men and their stock were dead. It was a great relief to many, and a further enrichment of their legendary status, when Jim Oldfield rode out of the desert alive and well.

Eventually, the mob reached permanent water. Jim credited Bill with getting the cattle through without losing a single beast. George Farwell pointed out that without Jim Oldfield and fresh horses, it would have been a much different story. However, the combination of two of the great stockmen of the region working together on such a risky undertaking was probably the key to their success.

It was perhaps fitting that the last mob to travel down the Birdsville Track, in 1968, was droved by Bill Gwydir. His descendants still live and work in the area; his grandson is head stockman on Adria Downs Station.

THE
LORD
OF THE
DESERT

While most stockmen handled cattle, horses and sheep, there was one group who literally stood apart. Cameleers were often discriminated against, and uniformly labelled Afghans although many came from what is now Pakistan and India. Yet they were stockmen to their long strings of camels that plodded slowly through the landscape. Throughout the nineteenth century and well into the twentieth they were an exotic presence throughout the arid outback regions. They also played a vital role in the development of outback infrastructure and yet they are frequently overlooked. No book on the stockmen of Australia would be complete without recognising their contribution. As with many other stockmen, few cameleers achieved fame for their efforts. However, one stands out. His name: Dervish Bejah.

Bejah, as he was known, was from Balochistan, a fiercely independent province in what is now Pakistan. When Bejah was born, probably in 1862, Balochistan was part of India and when he grew up he joined the Indian army, rising to the rank of sergeant.

By then the value of camels and good cameleers was well recognised in Australia. First imported to Tasmania in 1840, they were soon playing a vital role in exploration of the arid interior of the mainland. While camels were a feature of exploring expeditions, they soon became the backbone of the outback's supply networks. They carried drilling equipment into arid areas to sink wells along stock routes for cattle and sheep. They transported the comforts of civilisation to some of the loneliest stations in the outback.

Bejah responded to the demand for cameleers and left for Fremantle, Western Australia, in 1890. He was working in South Australia in 1896 when Lawrence Wells recruited him (and an assistant, Said Ameer) for an expedition 'Equipped at the request and expense of Albert F. Calvert, Esq., F.R.G.S., London, for the purpose of Exploring the remaining blanks of Australia.'

The blanks in question were in Western Australia's Great Sandy Desert and Bejah soon proved to be more than a good cameleer. At one point, Wells pushed the camels to breaking point, forcing them far into the searing wastes without food and water. By 24 August 1896, Bejah had had enough. Wells recorded in his diary, 'Bejah shepherded his camels until midnight, and then tied them up. This morning he would not eat any breakfast; and said, "Camel no eat, me no eat." The poor animals look like starved kangaroo dogs this morning.'

The tactful cameleer hadn't confronted the expedition leader directly, but he'd drawn a pretty clear line in the sand – if Wells didn't care what happened to the camels, he might think differently about human life. Wells makes no reference to what he thought of Bejah's attitude but the route he took that day says a great deal. He altered course 90 degrees. It wasn't a complete about-face, but it was a start. The next day he made another 90-degree correction and headed back towards his base camp.

On a subsequent foray, Wells's brother and another man deliberately separated from the rest of the expedition and perished from thirst after their camels strayed and they were too weak to catch them. The main body of the expedition only escaped the desert thanks to the efforts of Dervish Bejah.

After the expedition Wells was vilified in newspaper reports of the tragedy. History was much kinder on Bejah. His efforts to sustain the camels in his care were regarded as the reason a worse disaster didn't overtake every member of the expedition. At a reception for the survivors, given at Government House in Adelaide, Wells presented Bejah with the expedition's compass, a memento he treasured for the rest of his life.

Bejah returned to Marree (known at the time as Hergott Springs) and resumed his life transporting goods throughout the arid areas of South Australia, New South Wales and Queensland. For years he was a familiar figure on the Oodnadatta, Strzelecki and Birdsville tracks. In 1909, he married a Marree woman, Amelia Shaw, who bore him a son, Abdul Jabbar (who became known as Jack). He continued to work into the 1930s, his strings of camels competing with the encroaching motorised transport that found the rough outback tracks, sand dunes and occasional floods hard-going.

In the late 1930s, when washing machine magnate Alan Simpson funded an expedition led by Cecil Madigan to attempt the first crossing of the Simpson Desert (named in honour of the expedition's benefactor), Bejah was the obvious choice of cameleer. In August 1938, Cecil Madigan went to see him.

I found him the grand old man Larry Wells had always represented him to be, still full of tales of the great adventure of the journey of the Calvert Expedition . . . and proud to tell that Wells had called him his friend. Bejah said with great regret that he was too old to go [he was then seventy-eight], but his son Jack, who was away at the time, would go, and Jack was a good boy on whom I could rely. He had a big round up of camels to show me and there were obviously plenty to choose from. The only uncertain quantity was Jack, whom I did not see till the following February, when I made another trip to Marree for that purpose. Jack Bejah impressed me favourably at once. He was young, solidly built and powerful, and seemed keen on the undertaking. He had his own camel team which he used on stations and fencing jobs in the outback, and could make up the required number from his friends' herds in Marree, where there seemed to be a sort of pool of camels, mostly out of work. Jack was tough, knew camels and the country, and seemed just the man for the job. Indeed, he later thoroughly proved himself to be a worthy son of his father. He was one of the first members appointed to the party, and he could not have been a better choice.

Madigan met Bejah again when the expedition was about to start. Bejah's son had already set out with his camel team but Bejah made a point of going to see Madigan when his train pulled into Marree at six in the morning.

> He was very anxious to impress on me that we should never let the camels loose. 'Always have your camel in your hand,' he kept repeating, shaking his hand as though holding a nose-line to emphasise his point. It was not clear just how the camels were to get any feed. Bejah had had trouble with the camels getting away in the night during the Calvert Expedition, a thing that could be fatal.

In fact Bejah had seen two men die for just that reason.

Bejah retired around the time of Madigan's expedition, and dedicated himself to growing date palms. He was still living in Marree a decade later when author George Farwell met him while undertaking a journey up the Birdsville Track, researching his book *Land of Mirage*. It fell to Farwell to document the passing of the cameleers. Roads had improved and trucks had become more reliable. Large numbers of unemployed camels had been over-grazing Marree's common. The decision was eventually made to shoot the creatures that had once been the lifeblood of outback transportation. After they were gone many of the 'Afghans' returned to their villages in India and Pakistan. They'd spent their lives being treated as outsiders and felt there was nothing for them in Australia. Bejah, however, regarded it as home.

Farwell found the old cameleer still 'tall and aristocratic' although he was nearly ninety. Bejah took him to the town's mosque, a building made of tin. The interior was in stark contrast to the humble exterior. Beautifully embroidered prayer mats lay on the stone floor, images of Mecca hung on the walls. In the centre of the mosque the Koran was wrapped in silk. Most impressive of all was Bejah – reverent and dignified.

In his acclaimed 1954 film, *The Back of Beyond,* John Heyer briefly featured Bejah, who was then well into his nineties. The film showed him slightly hunched as he walked to prayer on a treeless bluff outside the town. He was described as the last of the lords of the desert. He was still turbaned, as he was when photographed with the Calvert Expedition nearly sixty years before, but time had turned his beard pure white and his face was deeply lined. The film's narrator translated his prayer – for contemporaries who had perished in the stony desert far from home. Soon the prayer was for him.

Bejah died in Port Augusta Hospital on 6 May 1957. With him the days of an extraordinary breed of outback pioneers drew to an end. They were men apart, but the end of their era didn't go unnoticed. Bejah's death was reported in newspapers from *The Mail* in Adelaide to *The Times* in London.

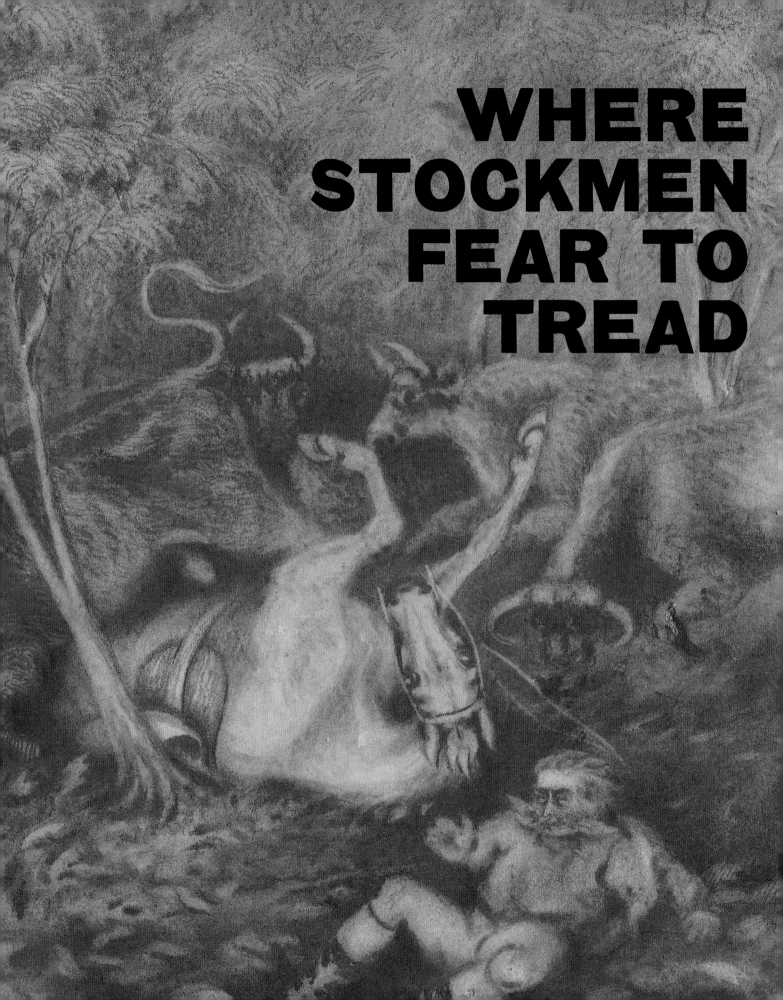

WHERE STOCKMEN FEAR TO TREAD

Among the many great stock routes that crossed Australia, one of the shortest was also the one that caused stockmen more worry than any other. It was only a couple of hundred kilometres long, a shortcut from the stations of the Northern Territory's Victoria River region to the Overland Telegraph near Newcastle Waters, but the Murranji (pronounced Murrun-jee) was a place where a drover could lose his reputation very quickly. It was a long narrow tunnel through bullwaddy and lancewood forests. Cattle that were accustomed to wide-open spaces were spooked by its close confines and frequently rushed in its depths. When they did, there was little hope of getting them back.

It was on the Murranji, in 1919, that stockmen set the record for what's thought to be the longest dry stage for cattle in Australia. According to Nat Buchanan's son, Gordon:

> One of the greatest feats of skilful handling in the annals of cattle-droving was performed on the Murrinji [sic] Track in 1919 by the Farquharson brothers. By covering without loss the longest dry stage, one hundred and ten miles [176 kilometres], ever recorded their bullocks broke the Australian record. This achievement may have been approached by smaller and therefore more mobile mobs, or when aided by parakeelya or other moisture-holding plants, but these cattle [more than 1000 bullocks] had no such advantages and no adventitious aid except cool and cloudy weather.

The Farquharson brothers – Hugh, Harry and Archie – were cousins of Gordon's, from Inverway Station. His account, written in 1933, is closest to the event in question and may have been obtained first-hand. However, according to authors Ernestine Hill and George Farwell, it may have been an even more significant feat than Gordon describes. They maintain that the trip took place in 1909 and was over 210 kilometres, effectively the entire length of the Murranji Track. The tale may have grown in the telling.

Nevertheless, in *The Pastoral Review* of 15 March 1952, George Farwell quoted Archie Farquharson, whom he'd interviewed shortly before his death in 1950:

> There was whips of feed. The big problem, of course, was water. Cattle going without water don't want too much feed. We had to take our plant of horses ahead of the mob to water them. We rode on to the Yellow Hole from the Armstrong, then went back for the cattle. Then we rode right on past the Murranji to the Bucket, watered them again and went back once more. The cattle were pretty quiet all the time, and they travelled well. Mind you, we had to watch them sharply. Double watch all the time. But we made that trip inside five days.

Previous spread:
Cattle stampeding through the bush, with a fallen stockman and his horse, mixed media, 1874, Adam Gustavus Ball, 1821–1882. A cattle rush was the thing stockmen fear most of all, as loss of life beneath the hooves of the galloping stock was commonplace.
(State Library of South Australia, B 63274)

Two stockman on the Great North Road, in the Northern Territory, rounding up a breakaway, 1969.
(Douglas Baglin, National Archives of Australia, B941: CATTLE BEEF/DROVING/MIXED/9)

According to the various accounts, the cattle were driven night and day. At night, a hurricane lamp was carried in the lead for the cattle to follow. One version has an Aboriginal stockman riding ahead with a board on his back to protect him from the heat of the lamp. Another account suggests the Farquharsons regarded their success as being due to night travel that reduced the moisture loss for the cattle and also gave them the opportunity to obtain water by licking dew from the feed they ate.

THE DEADLY MURRANJI

As with other stock routes in the remote parts of Australia, deaths were an all-too-common occurrence on the Murranji. There have been reports of up to twenty graves around the Murranji Waterhole, but the wooden crosses, blazes on trees and other signs have long since disappeared. In the *Pastoralists' Review* of 15 August 1912, 'H7H', the pseudonym for drover Hely Hutchinson, wrote of a crossing he'd done in 1905: 'The dry stage between Newcastle River and Yellow Waterholes is dotted with little brown mounds, sad witness to the awful fate that overtook the poor fellows whose mortal clay occupies them.'

Deaths among drovers, as a direct result of droving, appear to be fewer. Ernestine Hill and George Farwell both described the deaths of three drovers after a boss drover abandoned them. Hill's version was that three men – two whites and an Aborigine – were already suffering from fever (probably malaria) when the drover left them with food and a couple of drums of water while he pushed on with the cattle. The sick men were too weak to fend for themselves and the drovers with the next mob to come through found their remains. The boss drover became known across northern Australia as Murdering Charley.

One of the biggest problems with the Murranji was the fact that the track through the hedgewood was very narrow. In places where it had been hacked or burned through the scrub, mobs of cattle could end up being strung out over several kilometres. In such cases it was almost impossible to keep them together. If there were a rush, the cattle would be gone.

Everything changed with World War II, if only because it highlighted the need to improve the stock route in order to make it possible to move cattle beyond the reach of an invading enemy. Bulldozers tore a wide path through the scrub. The bores were improved. Maintenance trucks patrolled up and down the track throughout the droving season.

Despite the improvements, it was still a tricky place to take cattle. Drover Dave Allworth took the fourth-last mob of cattle down the Murranji Track in the mid-1960s. He told me about the various hazards along the way.

Yellow Waterholes is real drummy ground. If you galloped over it you could hear it drummy, and it was holey, you had to watch out. The only good thing on the Murranji is there's no stones there, so you don't get sore-footed bullocks. The Murranji is on a plateau; you go up a jump-up to get onto it. There's stone down the bottom but no stone there. Years gone by they bulldozed a track through. You had about 100 metres of sort of track going through and then you had solid lancewood or solid bullwaddy. You might go through four or five kilometres of solid lancewood or solid bullwaddy then you'd come out in a little bit of open forest area, bloodwood forest where it's a little bit thinner, and they're the places that you put your bullocks down at night. You could ride around 'em okay, and if you had a rush, you might have about 200 metres to put a bend in them before they hit the scrub. You wouldn't have more than that. It's tight.

'Look out on your left,' said McKenzie, 'the cattle are off like a streak! -
Rouse up the camp as you're passing' - his words seemed to end in a shriek.
And instantly into the saddle and out in the teeth of the rain,
We followed like fiends demented out e'er the soft Boree plain;
The splash of the hoofs through the gilgais and snapping horns far in front
As the mad cattle raced helter-skelter, solely our guide in the hunt.

Charles MacAlister, 'Cattle Rush on a Night Camp'

Travelling across the Murranji, boss drovers were always on edge, trying to ensure they didn't lose any cattle. Dave reckoned it meant losing a little bit more sleep. 'If you have a double watch,' he said, 'then the boss drover goes out there as the second man. If there's any trouble the boss might go through the night and not get any sleep whatsoever.'

A motor vehicle negotiates the Murranji Track, 1926. The narrow lanes of lancewood and bulwaddy meant taking cattle down the Murranji, especially those unused to confined spaces, particularly difficult.

(Carl E. Schultz Collection, Northrern Territory Library, PH0315/0040)

The threatened invasion of northern Australia by the Japanese in World War II saw the Murranji transformed in 1943 as a passage up to 400 metres wide was driven through the bullwaddy and lancewood thickets.

(Charles Abbott, National Archives of Australia, M10: 4/107)

During the day, the pressure didn't ease. With mobs travelling only a few days apart, there was nowhere to pull up for a day or two. Every mob had to keep to its schedule. Often there was a mob at each waterhole on the stock route.

The narrow track also meant constant vigilance was required to keep the mob confined to a small area.

You never let the bullocks string in the Murranji. You've got no control. People think you've got twenty people around the cattle but you'd only have three men on the cattle. You'd have 1200 to 1500 bullocks and you've got three men, you've got a horsetailer, you've got a cook – five men. That's the whole camp. You'd have a man each on the wing and a man on the tail.

Despite the challenges, Dave managed to get through five trips across the Murranji without a bad rush. While the drover's reputation was the primary motive in delivering all their cattle in good condition, there was also a cash incentive.

Vesteys [his employer] paid a bonus for 98 per cent delivery. I forget what it was but it wasn't terribly much. So any smart drover was picking up cattle and a few cleanskins practically from the moment they started – and I'm talking about western desert, not inside. From the day you leave Wave Hill, you're lookin' for cleanskins; they won't stand out. Then in the Murranji, watering on the bores, there's always been a few drovers who've lost a few. Not necessarily from rushes; you see a lot on the Murranji if there's been a rush up ahead. So you might get the odd one or two bullocks coming in at night.

The bloke on night watch would come and say, 'There's some bush cattle comin' in.'

I said, 'Let 'em come in, mate. We'll sort 'em out in the morning. Let 'em come and we'll see what they are. Don't let 'em out.'

If they've got a Vesteys brand they're quite acceptable. I've delivered over my number at Helen Springs [another of Vesteys' stations south-east of the Murranji]. Three or four over and they never queried it.

And the best thing about droving on the Murranji?

It's always a great moment to come out of the Murranji. You look down through the bullwaddy and you can see that open plain about half a mile [0.8 kilometres] away. And the bullocks are walkin' into water at No. 10 bore, which is out on the plain. It's the one occasion you can let 'em string

because they're only going to string out onto the plain. I'd tell the men on the wing, 'Just watch the lead and don't let 'em jog. Let 'em string.' The bore's about half a mile away. And as you come down you think, 'Gee. It's a big relief to get out of the Murranji.' And you know from then on you've got the Barkly Tablelands and you can look your bullocks over every night and if you get a rush you've got as much country as you need to get 'em and put a bend in 'em.

As detailed elsewhere, the development of road transport in the mid-1960s rapidly put an end to the glory days of droving. In 1962 the number of cattle that travelled the Murranji was 24550. In 1967, the last year the Murranji was used, that number was down to 2653 head.

The last Vesteys mob to go through from Wave Hill rushed. Three-quarters of the mob may have been lost. Some of the cattle turned up 160 kilometres from where the rush started. Shortly after, in June 1967, drover Noel 'Pic' Willetts took the last mob over the Murranji – 1390 head from Newry and Auvergne stations.

MUSTERING CATTLE

There is a pleasure in a mad gallop; or in watching the dawn of day on a cattle camp – to see the beasts take shape, and change from an indistinguishable mass of white and black into their natural colours; in the dead of night to find yourself alone with the cattle – all the camp asleep, perhaps only a red spark betokening the camp. I always, when I think of it, find something unearthly in this assemblage of huge animals ready at any moment to burst forth like a pent-up torrent, and equally irresistible in their force. When every beast is down, asleep or resting, just pull up and listen. You will hear a low moaning sound rising to a roar, then subsiding to a murmur like distant surf – or, as I fancy, the cry of the damned in Dante's *Inferno*. When the cattle are like that it is a good sign. But in the moonlight this strange noise, the dark mass of cattle with the occasional flash of an eye or a polished horn catching the light – it always conjures up strange fancies in me: I seem to be in some other world.

Barcroft Boake, 1889

A jillaroo on the tail of a mob of breeders on Headingly, Queensland, 2006.
(Scott Bridle)

KING
OF THE
DUFFERS

It was in 1870, while exploring country around Cooper Creek, that one of the outback's lesser known, but highly regarded, pioneer stockmen, John Costello, saw the first evidence of the most famous cattle-duffing episode in Australian history – the tracks of hundreds of cattle heading south-west for 700 kilometres. To Costello, the tracks looked highly suspicious as there were no stations in the direction the cattle were headed, and cattle duffers had tried to hide out on the Cooper at least once before.

In the mid-1860s, a duffer named James Harnell, who went by the nickname Narran Jim, had taken stock he'd stolen from the district around the Culgoa and Narran rivers across Queensland to the Cooper. Along the way he stole a number of weaners from Bulloo Downs Station as well. An alert Bulloo Downs stockman contacted the police and when Police Inspector Fitzgerald and eight Aboriginal troopers tracked Narran Jim and surrounded him while he was sleeping, the cattle duffer woke to find himself looking down the barrel of Fitzgerald's revolver – and at seven years in jail.

THE SWELL CATTLE STEALER

At school he had best thought to despise. Religion is a bore to him which he abhors. He once heard something of the Tenth Commandment, and ever since his aversion to church-going folks is most intense. Growing up in this way he becomes cruel, crafty and cunning. He knows the employees on the different runs, and often succeeds in making confederates. He is pretty well kept up with information. At this period he labours large in the bar of a public-house. He possesses a kind of eloquence in blasphemy. When drunk, he never divulges the secrets of the profession, and at the very time when an observer would think he was fast asleep, he is as wide awake as a dingo in the presence of an unprotected flock of sheep.

The Brisbane Courier, 1872

Costello also knew that while the south-west corner of Queensland hadn't been taken up by squatters, there were paths through the wilderness that led to South Australia. He'd pioneered the stock route that followed the Cooper and Strzelecki creeks back in 1867.

Costello had taken up land south-west of Quilpie and had 200 horses ready for market when he decided to take them to Kapunda, just north of Adelaide in South Australia. Costello had a reputation both as a stockman and for his ability to navigate his way through untracked outback country, and he took charge of the droving himself. The mob was made up of unbroken colts and fillies, and reputedly the young horses were in such good condition that they played up all the way to South Australia. There, as was the case with Hawdon and Bonney thirty years earlier, his feat was rewarded with good prices for his stock.

Now, in 1870, not long after John Costello returned to his station from his visit to Cooper Creek, Thargomindah's Police Inspector Gilmour paid one of his regular visits, whereupon Costello informed him of the suspect tracks. Like Costello, the inspector didn't know of anyone who had sent away a large mob of cattle, certainly not down the Strzelecki to Adelaide, and he too suspected cattle duffing.

It transpired that the cattle had been taken from Bowen Downs, whose lax station managers at first dismissed the suggestion that hundreds of their cattle might have been stolen. However, when they mustered the station at the end of 1870, they found they were down at least a thousand head.

In January 1871 South Australian police arrested a stockman from South Australia's Blanchewater Station in possession of cattle carrying one of the Bowen Downs brands. He maintained the cattle had been bought from a stockman coming down the Strzelecki. At the time, Blanchewater had been enjoying a particularly good season and had been keen to restock. When over a thousand head arrived unexpectedly on their doorstep and were offered at a bargain price, Blanchewater's manager was perfectly prepared to swallow whatever story he was told about their origins.

Eventually, New South Welshman Harry Redford was identified as one of the stockmen who had lifted the Bowen Downs cattle. He was arrested in Gulgong and extradited to Queensland. In Roma, his case caused a sensation. The prosecution had what looked like a watertight case against the man identified as the duffers' ringleader. However, the trial conducted in February 1873 resulted in a controversial verdict of 'not guilty'.

What helped Redford was the fact that he'd firmly established the viability of a new stock route to southern markets from the increasingly settled western Queensland. Men like John Costello had dispelled the bad reputation of the region he'd passed through, but it was Redford who shattered the illusions with his feat with more than a thousand cattle. The 'dead heart' of Australia was supposed to be an arid wasteland, but Redford followed a major flood down the Cooper and Strzelecki creeks and had been forced to make detours around waterlogged floodplains lush with fodder.

The case was certainly sensational due to the jury's verdict but its real significance was drawing attention to the realities of the interior of Australia. Harry Redford's legacy may have been to open the eyes of many to the potential in the far horizons of the outback.

DEATH OF A STOCKMAN

For many stockmen working on remote outback stations, the spectre of death is never far away. Even so, while driving the 80 kilometres between Alroy and Brunette Downs stations on the Barkly Tableland on a beautiful winter's day, it was hard to imagine that in 1893 stockman David McKay had perished travelling along the same route.

It was initially reported that David, two 'black boys' (locals aged anywhere between eight and eighty) and fourteen horses had perished. Searchers had set out from both stations to find them, hindered by a thunderstorm that had erased the missing men's tracks. Nevertheless, the search party found where the three men had taken the saddles from their horses and set them free. With the saddles was a note:

> Blue bush, November 8 – My Dear Hutton – I am dying here for want of water. The horses are also dying. If any are recovered please sell them and send the proceeds to my mother with my love. Pay Jerry Connolly £5 out of them. The horses are all done, and there is no chance of escaping from perishing. Write to my sister, Mrs. Higgin. Give her my love for all. Good-bye, old friend. I am off.
> – DAVID McKAY

A subsequent report revealed that David would have survived if he'd had enough respect for his Indigenous companions to let them decide what to do. The *Rockhampton Morning Bulletin* reported that when found, McKay's remains were covered by bushes, earth and a rug. It was surmised that the two men who'd been with him had waited until he died before going off to find water.

Grave of Henry Ventlia Peckham, known as The Fizzer, a renowned Northern Territory stockman turned mail contractor, who drowned in a flooded river in 1911.
(John Oxley Library, State Library of Queensland, 195921)

THE GREAT DROUGHT

FILLING WATERBAGS IN
BED OF THE MARANOA.

In 1894 a drought unlike anything that had come before gripped the outback. It lasted until 1903. Losses for stations whose stock were trapped were appalling. In an interview given to the *Advertiser* in 1914, the owner of Nappa Merrie Station, on Cooper Creek, John Conrick, detailed his experience:

> I was more fortunate than many others, for they had to abandon their holdings, and I was not quite reduced to that extremity. Still, I had to strain every nerve to save the situation, and for a long time was feeding horses and cattle on mulga and minnaritchie [a species of bush similar to mulga]. The latter only grows in the watercourses and the stock is fond of the leaves. During those terrible eight years, I lost 3000 cattle out of 4000 on the run, and about 7000 out of 12 000 sheep. Those that survived, as you might expect, were not very robust specimens [following the ordeal], but they soon picked up, and a couple of years after the drought broke one would never have credited, judging by the appearance of the country, that it had ever been in the deadly grip of those awful dry seasons.

Conrick's station was in the middle of the country opened up after duffer Harry Redford had droved 1000 head of cattle through it in 1870. Further north, Sidney Kidman tried to save 2000 bullocks by having them moved from Carcoory Station (now part of Roseberth Station) to Haddon Downs Station, at the top of the Strzelecki Track. All of them perished. Cadelga, in the same area, had been stocked with 24 000 sheep, 10 000 cattle and 300 horses. At the end of the drought there were 300 sheep, thirty cattle and a handful of horses. Cordillo Downs lost 59 000 out of 66 000 sheep. Arrabury lost almost all of its stock. Coongie Station, west of the Strzelecki on Cooper Creek, was left with 920 cattle from a herd of 19 000.

Shearers and stockmen found themselves trapped at shrinking waterholes. Jack Button recalled being camped on Cullyamurra Waterhole, on Cooper Creek. It was the last water left. He watched brumbies come in to drink then become trapped, too weak to climb the banks. He and the men with him killed bullocks and lived on their tongues, the only part of the animals still edible. When Cullyamurra started drying out, Button gambled his life and carried his swag down the Strzelecki, escaping the blighted country on foot.

On Lake Nash Station, stockman C.E. Gaunt wrote a first-hand account of the impact. It was a vivid, though not entirely accurate, description.

'Tragic news came up the river that Marion Downs was wiped out,' Gaunt recalled. 'Herbert Downs also, and the manager of Idamere [now Glenormiston], Lamond, wrote Jimmy Tyson, who owned Idamere at that time, asking for instructions.' Tyson replied, 'Hang on a long as you can. If no rain, save yourselves at the last moment. Ride away and leave 'em.'

When Idamere's waterholes dried up, the station's stockmen left 35 000 head to their fate. According to Gaunt, all the cattle perished. 'The drought hung like a great funeral shroud over a vast extent of country. Roxburgh and Carandotta, having the only permanent water, held out. Headingly Station, adjoining Lake Nash, lost eighteen thousand head in four days – perished.'

Every day, the heavy clouds of the wet season gathered, the sky darkened and thunder rolled across the parched landscape, but no rain fell. This was a time when the only way to move cattle was by foot, but for most it was far too late for that. Animals died in their thousands. At Lake Nash, with its substantial waterholes, the catastrophe unfolded more slowly. As water dried up, the cattle came to the Georgina River and gathered around Lake Nash. According to Gaunt, 'The lake assumed the spectacle of a huge burying ground for stock, a mass of liquid mud with hundreds of cattle packed in that oozy slime, bogged, dead and dying, with others roaming around the banks bellowing and maddened by thirst.'

At the time, there were roughly 15 000 head on Lake Nash, and it was decided that the station workers should take 4000 of the strongest up 120 kilometres of dried river channels to where there was still water at the Big Hole, on the Ranken River, at Avon Downs Station. Downstream from Lake Nash, the river was completely dry for 180 kilometres.

The next day, young Michael Costello and his men loaded drays with supplies and water from the homestead tanks. They saddled their horses, and then with considerable difficulty eleven men got the cattle moving away from 'that charnel house and lake of liquid mud'.

It was the height of summer, mid-January, with dry storms and hot winds whipping around them. The cattle seemed to sense they were being taken somewhere better, though it could hardly be worse. They walked along the dry riverbed all day and into the night.

Gaunt described their grim progress. 'It seemed as if there was a spirit in the lead that said, "Further still! Further still!" There was no need to put a stockman at the front of the mob as the cattle kept to the river's channels.'

Just after dawn the plodding beasts reached the confluence of the Ranken and Georgina, three-quarters of the way to the Big Hole. Nearby was the Austral Downs homestead, abandoned.

Gaunt said to Michael Costello, 'I'll ride over and see if there's any water in the tank at Austral.' To his great relief there were four tanks, all full. He then went to look inside the homestead.

'When I did I got the shock of my life. Inside the room was a big red bull, sitting down, as cattle do, when resting. I slammed the door quickly and

THE DROUGHT—SHEEP AT A DRY CREEK.

The Drought, wood engraving, 1878, Samuel Calvert (1828–1913). This poignant depiction captures the experience of stockmen droving sheep to a creek, to find only dead animals in its bone dry bed.
(State Library of Victoria, IAN20/02/78/25)

waited. Presently, very gingerly, I opened the door inch by inch and peeping in saw no movement. I soon found out the cause. The bull was dead. He must have been wandering around the house, probably smelt the water in the tanks, and possibly the door may have been open and he wandered in and in his dying moments had pushed the door shut.

Gaunt also found the door to the station store wide open, the store still fully stocked, everything left behind after the inhabitants had decided to leave the station and escape with their lives.

After watering their horses, the Lake Nash crew found the head of the mob was already 5 kilometres up the Ranken, still trudging on. As the fierce heat of the tropical sun beat down, stock at the tail were starting to drop and die. Yet the main body kept walking, silent but for a low moaning.

In the evening, Gaunt and another stockman, Mick Scanlon, rode 10 kilometres up the river to find the lead. As they did so, they saw cattle all along the mob dropping and dying, but those that could, kept walking. Strong bullocks were in the lead, and dangerous in their thirst-maddened condition.

As night began to fall, one of the bullocks spotted Gaunt and charged him and his horse. His horse was gored and fell. Gaunt was thrown from his saddle. Amid the ensuing chaos, Gaunt had no idea where he was in the mob but managed to make it to a tree. As he climbed up he shouted to Scanlon that he was all right and would spend the night in the safety of the upper branches.

He stayed in the tree all night as agonised, perishing beasts continued to stagger past below. Only when the first light of dawn silhouetted the trees to the east did he leave the safety of his perch. Gaunt quickly found his horse, which had died of its wounds. He took his saddle and continued up the creek on foot, covering 6 kilometres to reach the Big Hole, where the other men had made camp. The scene at the Big Hole was as distressing as that back at Lake Nash. Wrote Gaunt:

> Maddened cattle, some blind with thirst, moan[ed] and walk[ed] through the water, being too far gone to drink. Up the bank they went and wandered out on the downs. After the drought broke we found that some of them had wandered six miles [10 kilometres] out from the river before dying. The tail-enders drifted in and these represented the last of the living.

Other cattle were so desperately thirsty that they gorged themselves to death. Some were seen to collapse on the banks of the waterhole with water pouring from their nostrils. When the men counted the cattle that had survived the terrible ordeal, they found that only 500 head were left from the 4000 that had started.

The day had yet another tragedy in store for young Michael Costello. A charging bullock disembowelled one of his prized horses as he watched, powerless to do anything. It was too much for the young man. With tears streaming down his face, he went and sat behind a dray, head on his arms, and poured out his grief.

His heart may have been broken by that day's events, but not his spirit. He eventually became the station's manager, and spent, by his own account, up to seven straight years battling severe drought. When the drought broke, he and his men started the slow, hard process of rebuilding the station's herd.

THE STOCKMAN'S CHRISTMAS GREETING.

DROVING SHEEP AT CHRISTMAS

It was Christmas eve, I remember, and a furious wind had been blowing the whole day in our faces. Weary, begrimed and half-choked with the dust, with blood-shot eyes and sunburnt faces, the three of us sat, after having had a pot of tea and something to eat, our thirst half-quenched, each one by himself, with his back against the leeward side of the tree…Here and there moving columns of dust, grass and leaves, the result of whirlwinds, towered high in the air; whilst, close at hand, covered with ashes from the small fire, which, though lately kindled, had already burnt itself out, lay our kettle, frying-pan and pannikins, and the bag containing our gritty meat and damper. To complete the scene there were the panting sheep, and bullocks with protruding tongues; the close-on-setting sun bathing the landscape in a dull red light, suggestive of an eclipse. Altogether it was a melancholy camp that night.

E. M. Curr, *Recollections of Squatting in Victoria*, 1883

We cannot use the whip for shame
On beasts that crawl along;
We have to drop the weak and lame,
And try to save the strong;
The wrath of God is on the track,
The drought fiend holds his sway,
With blows and cries and stockwhip
    crack
We take the stock away.
As they fall we leave them lying,
With the crows to watch them dying,
Grim sextons of the Overland that
    fasten on their prey;
By the fiery dust-storm drifting,
And the mocking mirage shifting,
In heat and drought and hopeless
    pain we take the stock away.

In dull despair the days go by
With never hope of change,
But every stage we draw more nigh
Towards the mountain range;
And some may live to climb the pass,
And reach the great plateau,
And revel in the mountain grass,
By streamlets fed with snow.
As the mountain wind is blowing
It starts the cattle lowing,
And calling to each other down the
    dusty long array;
And there speaks a grizzled drover:
'Well, thank God, the worst is over,
The creatures smell the mountain
    grass that's twenty miles away.'

Banjo Paterson, 'With The Cattle'

A Reminiscence of Drought In Central Australia, wood engraving, 1886, Alfred Martin Ebsworth. This image reflects the descriptions of the scenes on Lake Nash in the Northern Territory in the great drought of 1895–1904.
(State Library of Victoria, PAC-10010195)

BEYOND THE MIRAGE

For those who dwell in Australia's cities, most of the outback is remote. For those who live in the outback, nowhere is more remote than the Canning Stock Route. Its 1440-kilometre length, from Halls Creek to Wiluna, in Western Australia, passes through the great deserts that had killed explorers on the Calvert Expedition as late as 1896. The biggest problem of all for drovers was that there was absolutely no law along that distance, except Aboriginal law. And as far as the desert people were concerned, the stockmen were trespassing.

The Canning was built so that cattle stations in the East Kimberley could take their cattle-tick-infested stock to southern markets without having to walk them through the tick-free western Kimberley. Alfred Canning established the stock route with a chain of wells in 1910. He was a man as dry as the country the stock route traversed. When the four-year project was finished, with the loss of one man speared in an Aboriginal attack, he communicated his success with typical brevity: 'Work completed. Canning.'

However, it soon became clear that the government had made no provision for maintenance. In addition, none of the wells had windmills, so water had to be raised by hand or beast, which made it slow to water cattle, limiting the number who could travel in a mob. Drovers had to carry everything needed for a trip of up to eighteen weeks, as there was absolutely nowhere to resupply along the entire route.

Unfortunately, the flaws in the route were yet to be appreciated by the drovers who attempted to use it. The first to take stock down the whole length of the Canning Stock Route was George McIntyre, with forty-two horses and two foals. He is thought to have travelled with a young Aborigine named Nipper. Only nine horses made it to their destination, Coorow, 275 kilometres north of Perth. The animals were sold for £90 – the cost of delivering them was £350.

In January 1911, drover James Thomson started down the Canning with a small mob of cattle. His partner, Fred Terone, was forced to pull out before they got onto the Canning proper due to an attack of 'sandy blight'.

Without his partner, Thomson was short-handed. When he got to the Canning he was soon struggling to water his stock. He decided to employ a local Aboriginal man named Franky, who in some reports was described as 'half-civilised'. Now part of the droving plant, Franky and his wife (Lidia) were allowed to remain in the drovers' camp at night.

What happened next made headlines around the country. In the first week of September 1911 many Australian newspapers carried versions of the following report, which appeared in the *Sydney Morning Herald*:

Previous spread:
The graves of stockmen James Thomson, Christopher Shoesmith and an Aboritinal stockman known only as 'Chinaman', who were murdered by local people on the Canning Stock Route near Well 37 in April 1911. The stock route was so remote it was months before their bodies were discovered.
(Battye Library, State Library of WA, b1997428)

Jackeroo Peter Barry shapes a horseshoe on the bank of a billabong at Stock Riders Camp, Nicholson Station, Western Australia. His anvil appears to be a conveniently shaped rock.
(Percy Spiden, State Library of Victoria, H2002.199/1290)

MURDERED BY BLACKS.

FATE OF TWO DROVERS.

POLICE IN SEARCH OF NATIVES IN CENTRAL AUSTRALIA.

PERTH. Wednesday.

Two cattle-drovers, Cole and Pennefather, arrived at Wiluna, in the North Murchison district, yesterday, from Hall's Creek, by way of the Canning stock route, and reported having discovered, on June 29, at No. 37 well, 450 miles [720 kilometres] north of Wiluna, and 450 miles from Hall's Creek, the bodies of James Thompson [sic], George Shoesmith, and a native employee, who left Hall's Creek, in the East Kimberley, last January, to overland a small mob of cattle.

The three bodies were found within a radius of 100 yards [90 metres] of the well, and were partly buried, the knees only showing above the ground.

Thompson's skull had been smashed in, apparently by a heavy weapon; Shoesmith had a fracture of the left side of the skull, and a spear-wound in the right side of the neck, and the body was also cut in halves.

The native boy's body, supposed to be that of an aboriginal known as 'Chinaman', who left Hall's Creek with Thompson's party, was dismembered, and buried about 10 yards [9 metres] from that of Shoesmith.

All three bodies were fully dressed, with the exception of boots, and it is believed the victims were murdered while asleep.

Thompson's diary was found near the stock route on June 28, about ten miles [16 kilometres] from the scene of the tragedies. The last entry bears the date April 25. The diary of Shoesmith was picked up in pieces near the scene of the murders.

The firearms, horses, and cattle were taken by the natives. The camels and horses were used by the natives until knocked up, and then shot. The cattle were dispersed. One rifle, badly damaged, was picked up near the scene of the murders in an abandoned native camp. A hundred miles [160 kilometres] north of this place Cole and Pennefather saw natives wearing European clothing.

No. 37 well is within fifty miles [80 kilometres] of where Stephen [actually Mick] Tobin, of the Canning survey party, was murdered three [actually four] years ago. The natives in this part are apparently most treacherous, and a menace to persons using the stock route. Thompson and Shoesmith were ex-police constables, and Thompson was the son-in-law of August Lucanus, hotelkeeper at Wiluna, where his son and wife are living. A strong police party is leaving Wiluna in search of the murderers, who it is thought will be encountered within 20 miles [32 kilometres] of the stock route, as the surrounding country is barren.

Australians outside of Western Australia may not have known much about the Canning Stock Route but after a report like that they weren't going to forget it in a hurry. The incident highlighted the route's sheer isolation. It was a place where, even in the twentieth century, stockmen could find themselves 700 kilometres from the nearest assistance, in an area where the Aboriginal population was demonstrably hostile. It couldn't have escaped the notice of drovers contemplating the journey that Thomson, Shoesmith and 'Chinaman' had been dead for two months before their bodies were discovered, and another two months had passed before news of their fate reached the world at large.

Sad and sultry leagues of silence, bounded by a shimmering sky,
Make a man feel very lonely, very small and very dry;
We would cry in desolation but we cannot shed a tear,
And the creaking of the saddle is the only sound we hear.
As we feel the dreary silence stealing o'er our senses dim,
We imagine we are sinking and would rather sink than swim;
And we have a vague, weird fancy that Death is hovering near,
While the ever-creaking saddle is the only sound we hear.

W. A. Woods, 'Where Silence Reigns'

The bodies of the dead were buried on the stock route and are among the loneliest graves in the outback. There were other attacks over the subsequent decades but none so serious as this. Nevertheless, one drover told this writer, 'It was a pretty wild place. There were no police and those Aboriginal people out there had no respect for white law. You had to be prepared for anything, and I mean anything.'

While the dangers of the stock route were widely known, they didn't stop Eileen Lanagan becoming the first woman to drove cattle down the Canning in 1940. Her husband, George, was taking 800 head from Billiluna to two stations near Wiluna, and despite warnings from the police and others, she was keen to experience droving first-hand.

Eileen went on the eighteen-week trip as cook, with a young Aborigine, Baroo, as her assistant. The party also included eleven Aboriginal stockmen, Eileen's husband and one other white man. Being the wife of the boss, Eileen was allowed two saddle bags for her personal items, instead of the usual one. In the extra bag she carried a pot of face cream, a diary and a revolver.

Fortunately, Eileen had no need of the gun. Her husband was well aware

of the tensions with the local population and was strict about not allowing them near his camps. Yet he was also sensitive to their needs, and after killing a beast for his men he left the remains for their enjoyment.

Eileen's adventure was one of only a dozen droving trips down the Canning in the thirty years up to World War II. In the years after the war only another twenty trips were made. Drovers from that era recall that the trip took around fourteen weeks, with the stock travelling down in winter. At times it was so cold that the drovers dismounted and walked beside their horses in order to keep warm. By that time, desert Aboriginal people were increasingly being employed as stockmen and their knowledge of the country made the going easier.

In 1959 George Lanagan took a mob of cattle, from Billiluna Station, down the Canning for the last time. It was the last great stock route to be opened in Australia, the longest and most remote, and it remained a wild and dangerous place throughout its history. However, in modern times, four-wheel drives regularly traverse the Canning on what is considered one of the iconic adventures of the outback. Many of the wells and gravesites have been restored or maintained by volunteers who travel great distances from around the country to do so. Today the Canning is one of the few ways to experience one of the largest wilderness areas in the country, much of it still Aboriginal land. It remains a monument to the courage and endurance of the stockmen who faced its great emptiness, with cattle, and got them through.

Harry Cogzell, a northern Queensland stockman, lifting 'Johnnie' cakes (a rudimentary substitute for bread) from the ashes at an overnight camp, 1961.
(National Archives of Australia, A1200, L39276)

DROVING CATTLE TO MELBOURNE MARKET

The passing of the large mob through the quiet streets of the city in the middle of the night must have attracted the attention of most. It is a rather striking incident. The pattering of some 3000 hoofs, the bellowing of the affrighted cattle, the excited barking of the drovers' dogs, and the wild cries of the men themselves, accompanied by an increasing fusillade of stock-whips, combine to form a scene which only the most stolid can regard with indifference.

Australasian Sketcher, 1873

THE LAST CATTLE KING

James Tyson may have been the first cattle king but the man who inherited the title has held it ever since. Both men had similar humble beginnings. Sidney Kidman was born on a smallholding in Adelaide in 1857. Sidney's father , the third son of his parents, George and Elizabeth Mary, died of bronchitis only six months after Sidney was born, leaving his mother pregnant. In 1863, his mother remarried, to a farmhand named Starr who spent most of his time drinking and fighting. As his older brothers had done, Sid left home as soon as he was able.

'I think I was 13 when I decided to clear out,' he told a newspaper many years later (*Adelaide Observer*, 5 September 1903). 'I got hold of a cheap horse and bound for nowhere in particular, and with practically nothing on my back and no money in my pockets, away I went … I gradually worked my way north until at last I struck the Barrier [range, in western NSW].'

He eventually found work near Poolamacca homestead, doing odd jobs for room and board at a bush shanty called German Charlie's. He chopped wood, and for a few pennies tended visitors' horses and equipment.

It was just a few months later that his brother George found Sidney a job, with a 'squatter' named Harry Raines. As Sidney told a newspaper interviewer for The Register in 1968:

I got a job with him at eight shillings a week to do as I was told. I used to sleep in the dugout, the coldest shop I was ever in. In those days people did not have big swags and a lot of bedding but just a rug. That was all I had. I had to get up early, as it was the only chance to get warm, and hunt up the saddle horses.

Sometimes I would mind the goats and sheep and have a look for any stray cattle or sheep for Harry. He would say they were his; it was all open country. After the big drought broke in 1869 a lot of cattle came over from the Flinders Ranges and any that Harry could get belonged to him. I was sent away with a bit of a rug and a little tucker in my swag to look for them scores of miles away.

Sidney learned a lot about survival thanks to a young Aboriginal man named Billy, with whom he shared the work around the camp. Soon Sidney was so skilful that Raines started to hire him out as a guide to the new settlers filtering into the area.

Sidney was a princely fifteen years old when he got a job with three of his brothers – Sackville, George and Fred – on Mount Gipps Station. His pay was ten shillings a week and for eighteen months he got to see how a proper station operated. However, when another young stockman was employed for a pound a week, Sidney protested, and was promptly fired.

He returned to German Charlie's shanty and got work tending Charlie's small herd of cattle for a pound a week. The herd was largely made up of strays and unbranded cattle that were wandering the bush. Some were completely wild, and Sidney gained valuable experience looking after up to a hundred cattle at a time. Soon he'd learned how to pick the herd's mood, which were the leaders and which the followers, and those that were troublemakers. Like all good stockmen, he paid close attention for the first signs of a rush, and headed it before it got out of hand.

By this time Sidney had already started trading in stock himself. On one of his trips he picked up a small mob of horses at rock-bottom prices. Back at the bush pub, German Charlie sold the horses for a solid profit, with a generous commission for Sidney. The youngster discovered there were better ways to make money than just chasing cows.

Not long after, the outback gave him yet another lesson in the life of the arid west. Drought descended on the entire western New South Wales region, forcing German Charlie to sell off his increasingly blighted cattle, and lay off young Sidney. What caught Sidney's attention was how desperate things became on the surrounding stations. All they could do was hope for rain, while their cattle lost condition. Soon, many faced ruin.

Meanwhile, Sidney had to make a living. Copper had been found at Cobar, and mining being a hungry business, beef prices in Cobar were high. So in 1875, the eighteen-year-old Sidney went into the butchering business. He rode to a station 130 kilometres from Cobar to buy cattle, then droved them back to the town for sale. Prices were good, but the 260-kilometre round trip took the gloss off. Not long afterwards, he switched to trading in horses. He was soon ranging from South Australia up into Queensland, building a business and a reputation for an impeccable eye for stock.

By the early 1880s Sidney was trading in any outback commodity that might turn a profit. In 1884, he asked Isabel Wright if she'd marry him, and she agreed. Asked late in life what was the best deal he'd ever made, he quickly answered: 'My wife. She's been my mate for fifty years.'

When the mines around Broken Hill started booming, Sidney knew that where miners were concerned it was all about getting in first. He partnered with his brother, Sackville, in a butchery at nearby Silverton. Sackville was the more cautious and astute of the two, a curb on his younger brother's instincts, but they thrived.

Prior to 1895, Sidney had only dabbled in property. He'd bought a home in Kapunda in 1884 when he married Isabel. Then, in 1887, at age thirty, he acquired Thule Station, a 184-square-kilometre block of open mulga flats and ridge country not far from Charleville, Queensland. He then took an interest in Cobbrum, a 215-square-kilometre adjoining run. The two properties were consolidated with a third, Oblong, to become Elverston in April 1890. However, he let the properties go in 1893.

Two years later, though, Sidney and Sackville's world changed greatly. By then, a financial crisis saw the banks closing down properties and trying to sell them off. The Kidmans, on the other hand, were cashed up. In 1895, with the prices of properties across the eastern states at rock bottom, the Kidman brothers started buying.

The purchases were anything but random. Some properties were purchased to fatten cattle for market, while others were breeding properties producing cattle to be fattened. A significant difference was that they also bought properties in between, to help move stock between the two. In this, Sidney's years in the saddle, and knowledge of the country, were invaluable.

His willingness to personally inspect properties also paid dividends when dealing with city owners who in some cases had never set foot on their investments. Not only did Sidney and Sackville get the properties cheaply, the terms of payment were often extraordinary. In many instances they paid a small deposit, took possession, then mustered the stock and used them to pay off the balance. In such cases the actual cost to them was a mere tenth of the already depressed value.

In a few short years Sidney and Sackville constructed chains of stations whose concept was, for sheer size, nothing short of extraordinary. It required an intimate knowledge of the outback that only a stockman could hope to achieve, and a set of phenomenal bush skills to bring it about. The chains extended from the Northern Territory and western Queensland down the Great North Road, across the Barkly, and down the Birdsville Track into South Australia and New South Wales, to the railheads that gave access to markets in Adelaide, Melbourne and Sydney.

Suddenly, though, the Kidman operation was dealt two devastating blows. The first came early in 1899. In March Sackville Kidman contracted peritonitis, and within a few short days, the infection killed him, aged forty-three. Then, as Australia entered the new century, drought took hold of almost the entire continent on a scale beyond any previous experience.

In building their chain of stations, Sidney and Sackville had hoped to make their operation virtually drought-proof. The plan was that if one place was stricken, they could move the stock to a station where the feed was good. Yet this was no ordinary drought. It had been dry since the brothers had started buying in 1895, but between 1900 and 1903 almost no rain fell in the vast western-Queensland catchment that fed what was becoming known as the Channel Country.

Ion Idriess, author of *The Cattle King*, puts Sidney's total losses at 35 000 head of cattle, but Jill Bowen, author of *Kidman*, disputes the figure.

Stockmen she has interviewed suggest the figure was more like 70000. And yet, Sidney survived. He clung tenaciously to every one of the properties that formed the basis of his and his brother's enormous chain-of-supply strategy.

There was no rest for the 46-year-old. He was still in the saddle, deeply tanned after years of outdoor life, riding thousands of kilometres to visit his properties, and to buy and sell anything with four legs – cattle, sheep, horses, even goats. He said in an interview with the *Adelaide Observer*

> People think I have been making money for years,'. 'They must remember that I had stations before the drought, and held them all through. I, however, took the precaution to handle my stock, to send those from the bad places to my stations that were better off. I like the bush country, and am more pleased to talk to a man carrying a swag than to your politicians … I would just as soon have a good square meal on a station as sit down to the best spread at an hotel.

In the ensuing years Sidney's empire grew until 'the kid who knew his way about' had interests in properties that covered an area larger than England, Scotland and Wales combined. All through he continued to travel around his properties on horseback or in a motor vehicle. While he made extensive use of telegraphic communications, it was no substitute for hands-on experience.

The Argus wrote in an obituary the day after his death on 2 September 1935:

> At the time of this death he controlled or had interests in 68 stations, embracing about 85000 square miles [220000 square kilometres] of country, and carrying about 176000 cattle and 125000 sheep. … Sir Sidney Kidman's properties stretch intermittently from the Gulf of Carpentaria to Adelaide … In some parts, it is said, Sir Sidney Kidman could ride for 600 miles [1000 kilometres] without trespassing.

THE AUSTRALIAN LIGHT HORSE

From the early years of the Australian colonies, it was found that any military or police force needed to ride in order to cover the great distances of Australia. Soon even infantry units were mounted, and from their ranks the Australian Light Horse evolved.

When Australian forces were sent to the Boer War, their value as mounted infantry was enhanced by the fact that the majority were stockmen or farmhands who could shoot, ride and rough it as well as or better than their South African enemy. After Australian and Rhodesian troops held out at Elands River against a much larger Boer force, Lord Kitchener remarked, 'Only colonials could have held out and survived in such impossible circumstances.'

The horses swept forward! The clatter of galloping hoofs echoed strange,
Along with the opening chatter of maxim-guns finding the range.
The rifles cracked fitful and ragged, the horses tugged hard on the bit,
And sometimes an animal staggered, but seldom a rider was hit.

We hurried for safety, for cover – tense-hearted, with never a warp;
And bullets strummed under and over like tautly drawn strings of a harp.
The Turks, in a wicked endeavour, were sniping with purpose to stem
The tide of a race I shall never forget – the Anzacs were swooping on them!

Edwin Gerard, 'El Maghara'

In World War I most of the battlefields weren't suitable for the use of horses. However, the Light Horse, unmounted, served with distinction at Gallipoli and on the Western Front. In the deserts of the Sinai, the Light Horse were involved in several spectacular and courageous engagements, culminating in the Charge of Beersheba, the last great cavalry charge in history. With a British force of 60 000 desperate to secure the town and its vital water supplies, on 31 October 1917, 800 Light Horsemen of the 4th and 12th regiments charged three kilometres across open ground to attack the Turkish and German defenders. They faced entrenched infantry, machine guns, artillery and two aircraft. The defenders were taken by surprise, not believing such a charge would ever be attempted, while the fast-riding horsemen made it difficult for them to find their range. The Light Horse took the town with the loss of only 31 men and in the process carved out an extraordinary place in Australian military history.

Overleaf: Thunder Of A Light Horse Charge. This image is purported to have been taken at the Charge of the 4th Light Horse Brigade at Beersheba on the 31st October 1917, but may have been a reenactment staged a short time after. Significant numbers of stockmen from all over Australia joined the Light Horse at the outbreak of war. (Australian War Memorial, oai:awm.gov.au:A02684)

THE
HIGH
COUNTRY

In a land of extremes, it should come as no surprise that Australia also has an alpine region, one that is larger than Switzerland. Although few of its peaks attain more than 2000 metres, the mountains that straddle the border between New South Wales and Victoria are home to a breed of stockmen admired throughout the land and immortalised in our most famous verse. Theirs is a proud tradition that reaches back to the time when they first ventured into the Australian High Country, as far back as the 1830s.

The first of them may have followed the Aboriginal people drawn each spring to the mountains to enjoy the protein bonanza offered by prolific numbers of bogong moths (*Agrotis infusa*). It's also possible that shepherds whose flocks were perishing during a drought around the Goulburn district were guided to the High Country by Aboriginal people who told them of lush pastures that were to be found even when the lowlands were parched.

True or not, the first recorded expedition, in May 1823, was led by Captain Mark Currie and Major John Ovens, and guided by a former convict, Joseph Wild, to the present site of Canberra and on to an immense treeless plain that local Aboriginal people called Monaroo or Maneroo. The fact that Joseph Wild was acting as a guide suggests he was showing Currie and Ovens country he'd already visited, so the gentlemen could 'discover' it.

No sooner had the explorers reported their discoveries than the squatters swooped, with the first sheep appearing in what would become known as the Monaro in 1825. From the earliest times, the High Country was no place for the faint-hearted, in every sense. When physician John Lhotsky travelled to the High Country from Sydney in 1834, he found himself in a frontier society – hard people living in primitive conditions. In *A Journey from Sydney to the Australian Alps,* he wrote: 'I have lived before under absolute monarchies and under commonwealths; here I found myself surrounded by absolute anarchy and lawlessness.'

Some grazing in the area around Kiandra is thought to have occurred around this time and droving to the high plains may have begun not long after. One of the features in what is now the northern Kosciuszko National Park is called the Port Phillip Gap, indicating that it was a key point for early drovers taking stock to the newly established Port Phillip settlement that would shortly become Melbourne.

The routes across to the western side of the mountains were hard on men and stock. The High Country was cold country, and storms descended swiftly, with little warning, at any time of the year. The dangers were documented in William Brodribb's *Recollections of an Australian Squatter.* For some years William was station manager at Coolringdon, between Cooma and the Alps. In 1848, he attempted to take some of his own sheep across the mountains, possibly to a property he owned near Gundagai. William knew he was taking a risk in crossing the mountains in late autumn, but he decided to chance it anyway. He recorded that he 'started in May with 1000 maiden ewes and three men, one an old man acting as guide (who professed to know the route), and three horses to carry our supplies, cooking utensils and blankets'.

They travelled for several days, covering a respectable 10 or 12 kilometres per day and crossing several tributaries of the Murrumbidgee River, which in the vicinity of Cooma loops south then north to skirt evocatively named peaks like Yarrangobilly, Nungar, Honeysuckle and Black Cow. Near the 1630-metre Yarrangobilly Mountain, 75 kilometres north-east of Cooma, William's luck ran out. He wrote:

> We reached what is called the 'Port Phillip Gap', about the centre of the tableland on the summit of the Alps. We were overtaken by a tremendous snowstorm; it commenced about 12 o'clock at night, and by daylight the ground was covered with snow six inches [15 centimetres] deep.

William's guide suggested they get moving early and push hard to reach the western edge of this so-called tableland, most likely Long Plain. Once they started descending, the guide reasoned, they'd drop below the snowline and out of danger. Unfortunately, as the day went on, the storm got worse. Wrote William:

> The snow became deeper and deeper every hour and it fell so thickly we could scarcely see 100 yards before us, and the guide lost his way. The weather was intensely cold, and as the night closed in we came to a final standstill under the side of a high and woody mountain.

Man and beast were exhausted. With their camp blasted by wind and any kindling dampened by the snow, they struggled to get a fire going. The beleaguered men used a couple of blankets to rig up a screen to block some of the wind and snowfall, then tried to get some sleep. Huddled for hour after hour, trying to gain some warmth from the flames, it must have been one of the hardest nights of their lives.

The snow fell all that night and throughout the next day, making it impossible to move. William was starting to doubt whether they were going to survive. He wrote:

> Our position became very dangerous; if it continued many hours longer nothing could save us from perishing. At daylight the snow was nearly two feet [60 centimetres] deep, consequently it was impossible to move the sheep, and as our supplies were getting short, it was necessary to determine

what had better be done. I made up my mind to leave the sheep where they were with two men, and make a search with the guide to make out 'Yarrangobilly Gap', from thence to a small cattle station down the western side of the mountains, and there procure some additional supplies. Fortunately I had a compass and watch with me, or, in all probability, we should have been lost altogether.

I knew our course ought to be due west, and my guide was taking me north; we rode in this direction for more than an hour, across the spurs of the main range. I requested him to alter our course to west; in half an hour we found ourselves on the water shed to the Tumut River.

'We are all right, sir!' William's guide exclaimed, perhaps with new-found admiration for the navigational skills of his boss. 'Any of these watercourses will take us to the stock station.'

Nevertheless, struggling through snow and fallen timber, it took most of the day to get there. The station was just a hut, occupied by a lone stockman whose nearest neighbour was 30 kilometres away, but William wasn't complaining. 'We enjoyed a quart-pot of tea, damper, and salt beef, with a great deal of relish.'

It was certainly not the last time a High Country stockman would be glad of the sight of one of these huts. In fact, William hadn't been there long when another traveller appeared:

The poor fellow had been five days without any food. He lost his way in the mountains, and he had to abandon his horse, and for two days he carried his bridle and saddle; he became so tired and weak that he had to leave these articles behind. It was merely accident he made the hut.

The following day the weather started to clear, although the snow still lay deep on the ground. It ended up taking two days to get the sheep back to the stockman's hut, 'all safe'.

By 1854 William had prospered so much from fattening sheep for the Melbourne market that he was able to purchase his own 600-square-kilometre property, Wanganella Station, near Deniliquin. However, the High Country still stood between William and Wanganella, 400 kilometres to the west.

Having sent his family and much of their belongings the long way around, via Yass, 200 kilometres north, William set off with twenty saddle horses, five packhorses and sixty-five unbroken mares, fillies and colts. He picked up a mob of cattle and sheep from the station of a man named Brooks, and a guide to show him a route referred to as 'the way over the Snowy Mountains by the Murray Bogong to the head of the Murray'. It was believed

that the route had been used just once to drove cattle, possibly by the Ryrie brothers – William, Donald and James – overlanding 250 cattle to Port Philip in 1837.

Setting out in early January 1855, William had no idea what he was getting himself into. Afterwards, he was to reflect 'a dreadful route it is'. From a Ryrie station at Jindabyne, it tracked through the heart of the Alps, past 2068-metre Gungarton Mountain and 2061-metre Mount Jagungal (also known as Big Bogong) to the Tooma River, then down to its junction with the Murray Valley at another station, Walaragong (Welaregang), owned by John (later Sir John) Hay. In a straight line it was 75 kilometres, but William estimated the actual journey to be more like 250 kilometres.

His team consisted of six stockmen to help him drive the cattle and horses, plus an overseer named Nicholls and two men to take care of the sheep. The number of livestock isn't clear.

The first two days were relatively easy, but in the rough terrain William found it difficult to keep the stock together. In addition, he wrote:

> My men were young, and greenhorns for driving cattle. I had to be doubly active day and night. I had a magnificently strong little horse under me; he was wire itself, and he stood well to me all through the journey. After crossing the main Snowy Ridge (at this period of the year very little snow is on the mountains), we had to cross a table land, mountainous, and in many places very slushy for about 30 miles, and very boggy; and in every valley a running stream. Some portion of this country is heavily timbered, other portions open country and rocky; but all well grassed. None of it is occupied; the squatters are afraid of the snow in the winter.

William's high regard for his mount, Hector, may have been due to the constant work both horse and rider put in while crossing the High Country. Nearly every day, William needed to ride back to guide and help the shepherds, whose flock was struggling to keep up with the faster-moving cattle and horses.

There were one or two nights when the sheep didn't reach camp and had to be camped separately. After the sheep were settled, William and Hector still had to ride on to the cattle and horse camp, for as William put it, 'they required my personal attention by night'.

After 'many difficulties' in what is some of the most rugged mountain wilderness in Australia, William reached the western slopes of the High Country. There he was presented with the extraordinary view of the lowlands stretching for close to a hundred kilometres out to the western plains. Closer at hand, he wrote: 'I could see the valley of the Hume [the Murray]

HORSE POWER

William Brodribb's description of his 'strong little horse' suggests that in his time the qualities of the mountain horse that Banjo Paterson would describe in 'The Man from Snowy River' were already being appreciated. Paterson described the animal as:

> … a small and weedy beast,
> He was something like a racehorse undersized,
> With a touch of Timor pony – three parts thoroughbred at least –
> And such as are by mountain horsemen prized.
> He was hard and tough and wiry – just the sort that won't say die –
> There was courage in his quick, impatient tread;
> And he bore the badge of gameness in his bright and fiery eye,
> And the proud and lofty carriage of his head.

Paterson was certainly right in suggesting that a mountain horse is not much to look at, particularly to anyone unschooled in the finer points of equestrian conformation, but ride one up a steep mountain and it will make a lasting impression long before you arrive at the summit. A mountain horse is the four-wheel drive of the equine world, and can climb just about anything. They can certainly negotiate terrain that would thwart a trail bike, which is why horses are still the dominant mode of transport in the High Country today.

"RUNNING IN" HORSES FROM THE BUSH.—SEE PAGE 146.

The Man From Snowy River, watercolour, 1890–1905, Charles Hammond (1870–1953). This image was directly inspired by Banjo Paterson's poem.

(State Library of Victoria, H2004.31/5.)

meandering down 30 miles [40 kilometres] off – it appeared a deep abyss.'
Getting down there proved to be a major challenge:

On coming to the falls of the Hume, the mountains I had to descend were
very precipitous and rocky, and the first mountain more than one mile [1600
metres] to its base; and it was impossible to drive down the whole lot at
once. We had to cut off about 25 or 30 at first. I forced them down some 300
or 400 yards [275 or 365 metres], to the first ledge of the mountain; leave two
men on horseback with these, while I and the others went back for some
more; and so continued until we had the cattle forming a long line to the
bottom. All this was attended with much trouble and difficulty, and many
of the cattle injured their shoulders, particularly the large bullocks, and
some never recovered. Well, at last we reached the bottom of the mountain,
a deep valley, thickly timbered, with plenty of grass. The men, cattle, horses,
and myself were very much tired; in fact, I was nearly knocked up. Notwith-
standing, I had to walk up this steep mountain, leading my horse, for the
purpose of assisting the sheep down, and before we got these down to the
cattle I was fairly done up, and yet I must, as leader of the party, take my
watch during the night. I was truly tired of the journey.

It's not hard to see why William's men and colleagues thought so highly
of him. Not only would he never send a stockman to do a job he wouldn't
do himself, he evidently did more than his fair share. From start to finish,
the trip from the eastern side of the High Country to his new property took
nearly a year, during which time he never saw his wife or children. He wrote
of their first seeing each other:

O, what pleasure it is to meet those you dearly love! Who have been parted
from you for months, and after all the trials and difficulties and dangers
of a stock expedition of some hundred miles [160 kilometres] across those
Australian Alps.

By the mid-1850s other graziers were sending cattle to the High Country
every year. The fear of winter snows prevented permanent settlement, but
from October to May the mountain pastures offered relief grazing during
drought periods. They were soon seen as a supplement to the home station's
available feed supply, allowing increased stocking rates.

Until the late 1880s the practice was largely unregulated. However, in 1889
the New South Wales Government amended its land act to allow the first
snow leases to be issued. By the 1930s most of the High Country was covered
by such leases, and mountain huts were to be found from west of the newly

established Canberra, at the northern end of the Alps, to Omeo in Victoria.

Photographs taken in the 1920s, when grazing was at its height, reveal hundreds of cattle watering at the lakes around Mount Kosciuszko. In earlier times sheep had grazed the High Country as well, but predation by dingoes, especially on sheep left unattended, took such a toll that cattle were generally preferred.

At the end of each summer much of the High Country was set alight to burn off the grasses left uneaten by the cattle, promoting new growth for the season that was to come. In some cases it was Aboriginal people who conducted the practice, some of them having swapped their spears for spurs to join the stockmen. They were maintaining the burning regime they'd been following for thousands of years, and passing it on to their European colleagues.

Other Aboriginal people came to the High Country from further afield. Around the turn of the last century, a Queensland Aborigine named Skerry was horsetailer for a mob of store bullocks that were driven to Bringenbrong Station. After they were delivered, Skerry stayed. According to stock agent Harry Peck, 'Skerry was a wonderful rider. Mustering in bush country no one could pace him through timber and scrub.' One of the owners of Bringenbrong, Peter Mitchell, held Skerry in such high regard that he made provision in his will for Skerry's upkeep for life.

Getting to and from the High Country was still a difficult undertaking. Routes climbed many steep ridges – Corryong, Tumbarumba and Talbingo in the west; Omeo and Benambra in the south; Adaminaby and Dalgety in the east; Tharwa, Brindabella and Tumut in the north. In many places, stock ascended over 1000 metres to the summer pastures. Many of the stock routes were evocatively named – Jacob's Ladder, the Devil's Staircase – as were the peaks that surrounded them: Mount Terrible, the Fainter and the Pilot.

Perhaps the toughest stock route of all was Hannell's Spur. It was a true 'one miler', a vertical ascent of over 1600 metres, from the Geehi Flats on a tributary of the Murray River at 500 metres to the pasturage around Mount Kosciuszko at 2200 metres. The explorer Paul Strzelecki had travelled the route as early as 12 March 1840, when he became the first to climb Kosciuszko, which he named and declared to be Australia's highest peak. Of the climb he wrote: 'The steepness of the numberless ridges intersected by gullies and torrents rendered this ascent a matter of no small difficulty.'

Taking cattle up the spur was even harder. Originally, it was impossible and livestock were taken by a circuitous route through the Tom Groggin Flats, then up to Dead Horse Gap and onto the Rams Head Range, a loop of about 20 kilometres. The direct route, almost straight up, was only 10 kilometres. First, though, a track had to be cut. In the 1920s, Kerry Pierce, who owned or

Hereford cattle near Kiandra
in the Snowy Mountains
caught by heavy snowfalls
late in the summer grazing
season, May 1957.

(W. Pedersen, National Archives of
Australia, A1200, L22767).

partly owned North Greg Greg and Bringenbrong stations, teamed up with Alf Hannell, another partner in Bringenbrong, to get the work done. A local stockman, Leo Byatt, chose the route.

In a collection of oral histories of the Snowy Mountains, another stockman, Errol Scammell, recalled its construction and use. Local men were paid a pound per day, good money at the time, to cut a 2.5-metre-wide passage through the scrub and snow gums, straight up the spur. Where the track emerged from the scrub into the open alpine pasture they formed what became known as Byatts Camp.

Scammell remembered that stockmen had great difficulty forcing cattle up the steep track. The beasts didn't like the narrow passage and the steep climb. Stockmen cut out twenty head at a time and forced them up, hoping the rest would follow. If they didn't, the next stockman would start another twenty, pushing them all the time. When the small mobs tired, the stockmen would leave them part-way up the climb and go back for more.

Tourists as well as stockmen used the track. Visitors to the mountain huts and cattle camps soon discovered a remarkable breed of stockmen. Many of them spent from October to May living in the High Country, far from the comforts of civilisation. They endured almost complete isolation during those months, and whatever the elements threw at them. Yet they also had some of the most ruggedly beautiful scenery in the country literally at their feet. Over summer, the pastures where the cattle grazed became meadows covered in wildflowers. At night the sky was lit with stars that sparkled like diamonds. The names they gave the high plains reflect the beauty that surrounded them – Town of Roses, Plains of Heaven, Ryrie's Parlour.

Little wonder the exploits of the High Country stockmen became the stuff of legend. Eventually, a composite of people writer Banjo Paterson met during his travels in the High Country and the Monaro formed the basis for what is now Australia's best-known poem. Paterson met one of the men specifically credited with being the inspiration for 'The Man From Snowy River', Jack Riley, on a visit to the Australian Alps in 1890, just weeks before the poem was first published in *The Bulletin*.

The Irish-born Riley had worked on stations on the Monaro and western sides of the Alps and was approaching the age of fifty when the poet visited him in his remote bark hut at the foot of Mount Kosciuszko, on the Murray River Flats at Tom Groggin. Paterson spent the night listening to the tales of Riley's adventures in the mountains and on the Snowy River, where he had once lived. The next day Riley took Paterson up the stock route to the main range via Leatherbarrel Mountain and Dead Horse Gap (the approximate route of the road now called the Alpine Way).

He hails from Snowy River, up by Kosciusko's side,
Where the hills are twice as steep and twice as rough,
Where a horse's hoofs strike firelight from the flint stones
    every stride,
The man that holds his own is good enough.
And the Snowy River riders on the mountains make their home,
Where the river runs those giant hills between;
I have seen full many horsemen since I first commenced to roam,
But nowhere yet such horsemen have I seen.

Banjo Paterson, 'The Man From Snowy River'

There are many stories of Riley's expertise as a rider and guide to the High Country, where he spent his entire adult life. Greg Greg stockman Tom Evans recalled mustering stray bullocks with him on Leatherbarrel Mountain:

Old Jack says to me, he says, 'See 'ere now, young feller. Youse goes that away and wees goes this way.' And off they went leaving me to look for the bullocks on my own. I was only a bit of a kid and I did not know the country and I was scared I'd get bushed, and I had a hell of a job getting through the big snow-drifts in the gullies, and I was having a hell of a time when I walked right onto the missing bullocks camped right against a big snow-drift. They were wild as hawks and my horse was a bit knocked up and had a shoe loose by this time, and it was a good time after dark before I got the brutes down to the mustering paddock at Groggin. Old Jack and the others won't believe that I have got the bullocks all on my own, but the next morning when they wake up here they are, and old Jack says, 'Looka here now, they needs a boostin'.' And with that he after them and into them with his whip, and there were no two ways about it, he could ride like the very devil, and he stayed with those bullocks no matter what they turned and did, and the whole time he was cussing them and taking pieces off them with his whip. They got boosted all right.

Another story, attributed to John Pierce in the *The Argus* and reprinted in *The Corryong Courier* of January 1949, comes close to the exploits of the man from Snowy River:

A station-bred horse, gone wild, was running on the Leatherbarrel Mountain, on the road to Kosciuszko from Groggin. The horse had defeated every attempt to catch him, although all of his 'running mates' had fallen victim to the stockmen's strategy…So a council of war was held and a plan of campaign devised to trap the outlaw. A yard was built in a strategic position across tracks near a creek that the horse habitually crossed, and duties were assigned to each member of the chase.

It was as though he had sensed our plan. As he flashed down that cliff – it was little less, anyhow – we didn't think any man could follow him down. But John Riley pulled his hat down over his ears, and with a wild yell charged down after the outlaw while his friends held their breath. Riley vanished from sight in a flurry of heels and a shower of dirt – and hardly a man among the hunters thought to find him alive.

More circumspectly, the others made their way down to the trap-yard across the creek trail. There, to their amazement, was the horse, yarded and winded, and there too was Riley – coming back up the slope. Riley was not very talkative about what had happened from the time he disappeared from view until the time he ended his chase. But he did vouchsafe the hint: 'See here, now,' he said. 'I went so fast down the slope the wind got in me eyes and the tears blinded me.' And, blind, he had ridden past the yard, into which the quarry had careered head long, and was unaware of the capture until his breeze-tortured eyes had cleared.

Riley lived in his hut at Tom Groggin until he was in his seventies. By then his employer, John Pierce, realised Riley was no longer able to look after the cattle. He appointed a new overseer, Fred Jarvis, with instructions to keep an eye on Riley as well. Then, in 1914, as winter approached and the cold around Tom Groggin grew more intense, Riley was taken ill.

As *The Argus* reported on Friday, 17 July 1914: 'Word reached Corryong on Saturday [11 July] that his condition was serious, and some of his friends decided to bring him to Corryong to the hospital.'

Kosciuszko guide Will Findlay told local author Tom Mitchell:

He'd been pretty sick once before, and had been away with that disease where your legs all swell up, you know, dropsy – but he was cured and had come back to his hut in Groggin. I was out there mustering cattle all round those hills with three other men, and I called in to see old Jack and found him pretty bad. I said we would take him into Corryong to the doctor but he said no, he'd rather stay there. So we left him, and we went on with the mustering. A few days later we looked in again and here is the poor old fellow lying on the floor just about at the end of his tether. So we knocked together a bit of a stretcher out of a couple of saplings and some hessian that was kicking around the hut, and we set off to carry him in to the doctor.

The original Man from Snowy River, Jack Riley, in the door of his hut at Tom Groggin, on the headwaters of the Murray River.
(Corryong Historical Society)

The Argus listed the other men with Findlay – A. McInnes, J. McInnes, Bob Butler, and the overseer Fred Jarvis.

About half-past 9 o'clock on Tuesday the party left the Groggin Hut, carrying Riley on the stretcher, the men taking turn about at the handles and leading packhorses with provisions and blankets. The first four or five miles [6 to 8 kilometres] from the valley was covered without much difficulty, but when it became necessary to climb out of the gorge over the shoulder of the Hermit Hill [now known as Hermit Mountain] the real difficulties began. The track ascends through wild scrub and rocks over 2000 feet [600 metres], and the party soon found that the task was beyond them. To make matters worse, snow began to fall, and the cold became intense.

Tom Mitchell also described the scene.

Jack Riley, his spirit hovering between this world and the one just a little beyond us all, lay silent, or shouted sporadic bursts of words mingled with queer sounds. Snatches of song, strange names, imprecations, sighs, terms of endearment, yells of encouragement, or warnings to unseen men, all came tumbling forth, sometimes with startling clarity, sometimes just a babble of incoherencies.

The grave of Jack Riley in Corryong, Victoria, 2004.
(Michelle Havenstein)

The men found they were unable to manoeuvre the laden stretcher up the steep and narrow track that ascended Hermit Mountain, which at that point flanks the Murray River with almost vertical slopes known as the Murray Gates. Almost at a loss as to what to do, the mountain men turned to their horses. As Tom Mitchell wrote:

Bob Butler was the smallest and lightest of the party, and he jumped up onto the quietest of the horses and poor old Jack was lifted up into the saddle. Bob held him there with his arms round the thin waist. The horse, panting and straining, was led and pushed inch by inch up the mountain. At the top the weather was blowing a bitter gale, with flurries of snow stinging down through the straining trunks of the forest. Jack Riley's head slumped and they thought that he had gone, but he rallied as they began to pick their way through the fallen timber on the descent.

They reached Hermit's Creek in late afternoon. There, according to Mitchell:

They offered him a drink of his beloved whisky, but to their surprise he refused, saying that he could not swallow it. 'Cripes, he must be crook!'

someone remarked. 'If we can get him to the hut at Surveyor's Creek, we can get him into a bunk and warm him, and he'll be all right,' was the common opinion.

Reported *The Argus*:

> The stretcher had then to be brought into use again, and just at dark the party reached Surveyor's Creek Junction, where a deserted mining hut provided a shelter for the night. Mr Jarvis went up the creek to the tin mine, and arranged for assistance in the morning, and the others made a fire and installed the patient as comfortable as possible in front of it. He seemed to rally a little, and spoke to his friends, but the weakness reasserted itself, and shortly afterwards he suddenly swayed and died.

Jack Riley's spirit stayed in his beloved mountains, but his body was carried out the next day, strapped to the back of a packhorse. He was taken to Corryong, where he was laid out on a billiard table in the Coffee Palace, a local emporium, before being buried in Corryong Cemetery on 16 July 1914. His gravestone now reads: 'In Memory of THE MAN FROM SNOWY RIVER'.

Was he or wasn't he the man from Snowy River? Without doubt, he was the kind of stockman Banjo had in mind. And just as Banjo wrote of his hero, years after Riley's death there were plenty of stockmen still telling stories of his rides. He was one of the best. In its obituary *The Argus* recognised as much:

> Familiar with every inch of "Head of the River Country" he has given willing assistance to numbers of tourists passing through, and was better known than probably any other man on the mountains. A fearless and dashing horseman in his young days, a first-class hand among stock, and an Irishman, open-hearted and generous, he was liked and respected by all who knew him. In bushcraft, even among the experts of the Murray, Gippsland and Monaro, he stood alone.

While highlighting the horsemanship of High Country stockmen, Paterson's poem also drew attention to the grandeur of the High Country. Increasing numbers of visitors were drawn to admire the scenery, hike its giant hills or ski its winter slopes. However, those who came expecting wilderness found herds of cattle grazing the summer pastures or autumn fires lit by the drovers to burn off the dying snow grass and promote new growth in the autumn.

By the 1930s concerns were growing that the amount of grazing and burning on the summer pastures was damaging a fragile environment that was unique in Australia. Many stockmen appreciated the need to keep stock off fragile areas, but didn't believe they should be excluded from the High Country altogether. Nevertheless, over the ensuing decades almost all of the snow leases in Australia's High Country were terminated. A Victorian Government task force in 2005 recommended the last of that state's snow leases be ended. With regard to the loss of the 170-year history, heritage, skills and knowledge of High Country stockmen, the task force concluded: 'The mountain cattlemen's tradition is maintained and celebrated in a variety of ways outside the park, including through books, poetry, films and festivals.'

This assumes culture isn't a way of life and set of values experienced first-hand. Or as Banjo Paterson put it in his poem 'The Daylight Is Dying':

> Beyond all denials
> The stars in their glories
> The breeze in the myalls
> Are part of these stories.
> The waving of grasses,
> The song of the river
> That sings as it passes
> For ever and ever;
> The hobble-chains' rattle,
> The calling of birds,
> The lowing of cattle
> Must blend with the words.

The western falls of the Snowy Mountains, 2012, involving vertical ascents of up to 2000 metres to reach summer grazing.
(Michelle Havenstein)

Visit the High Country today and you'll find little of its living cultural heritage, whether Indigenous or High Country stockmen. You won't wake before dawn as the horses are saddled in preparation for a day spent mustering. You won't meet stockmen skilled in leathercraft, horsemanship and survival in the bush. You won't see cattle driven down mountainsides that trail bikes would find impassable. You won't meet people whose heritage reaches back in an unbroken chain to the first settlements in and around the High Country, people who for months of the year lived in such splendid isolation that they regarded themselves as being truly free. And yet their greatest feat of endurance may be that, although they're gone, they remain one of the pillars of our national identity: the High Country stockmen.

THE HIGHLANDS

Along the southern side of the high tableland of Monaro plains, there
is a range covered with perpetual snow, at whose feet runs the Snowy
River, a small stream in winter, but a large river during the melting of
the snow in summer.

[A high country stockman], after three weeks' trying, got across
the shoulder of the mountains, and then came back to take the cattle
into the fertile country beyond. He kept his route secret, only mark-
ing the trees at intervals, but during the time before he returned,
there were a dozen different settlers searching for his tract.

David Lindsay Waugh, *Three Years Practical Experience
of a Settler in NSW (1834–1837)*

STOCKWOMEN

The outback abounds with the stories of stockmen whose feats of endurance, courage and resourcefulness have become the stuff of legend. Yet discovering the legacy of stockwomen is more challenging. Sometimes their contribution is only hinted at. Sometimes it's deliberately skirted. Yet women were there, behind the stock, in the stockyards and in the camps. Many were as good as the men. Some were even better.

> And often travellers such as I
> Had seen, and thought it strange,
> A woman working on the line
> That crossed McKinlay Range.
>
> Had seen her in the dreary wake
> Of stock upon the plains,
> Her brown hand quick upon the whip
> And light upon the reins.
>
> Mary Durack, 'Red Jack'

In *Flynn of the Inland,* Ion Idriess referred to John Flynn visiting an unnamed station, 'the home of the Five Sisters', when he was a patrol padre in the 1930s, travelling by camel around the outback. Two of the girls explained to him that the other three, 'Jess, Bess and Tess', were 'out on the run rounding up cleanskins with Dad'. Idriess added: 'The father had practically forgotten his only disappointment: just occasionally with wonderment he realised that his "boys" were girls.' According to Idriess:

> They could ride any horse on the run, break in any 'outlaw' and enjoy the taming; could ride from dawn till dark on a muster for a month on end and find only joy in it. They had galloped before the thunder of a cattle stampede in the dead of night, had swum flooded rivers while clinging to their horses' tails.

The reference to girls as boys is far from unique. Catherine 'Kate' Buchanan, wife of legendary drover Nat Buchanan, was described in similar terms while working on Mihi Creek Station, which was managed by her father. According to her son, Gordon: 'John Gordon, my grandfather, used to say long ago that "my boy Kitty is the most intelligent worker on Mihi Creek and my right-hand man".'

Previous spread:
An unnamed woman droving cattle on the Great North Road, 1923.
(State Library of South Australia, SLSA PRG280/1/41/271)

Stockwoman Bridgette Bouma from Paterson's stock camp (contractors) loading weaners onto a road train, Headingly,Queensland, 2011.
(Evan McHugh)

The gender confusion may have typified the prejudices of the time, but in its way it was the ultimate compliment a bloke could give. If a woman was doing the work of a man, and doing the job as well or better, she was considered to be a man, or as good as.

White women may not have received much recognition as drovers or stockmen, but even less value was placed on the contribution of Aboriginal women. When George Farwell visited Clifton Hills Station in the late 1940s, he focused on renowned stockman and station manager Artie Rowlands. However, he does refer to Artie's Aboriginal wife.

> Mrs Rowlands was a good mate for him, since it was her country, too. Born at Mungerannie, she was descended from the Dieri tribe through her mother, and was widely reputed to be as good at handling cattle as a man. For many years she rode out to the cattle camps with her husband, though latterly she was obliged to remain at home, because the Flying Doctor network insisted that someone be at hand to look after the radio.

Songwriter and author Ted Egan recognised the presence of Aboriginal women in his song 'The Drover's Boy'. The 'boy' turns out to be an Aboriginal woman who is killed when her stockhorse bolts and she suffers a fall. The gender mutation also conceals a relationship between the drover and the woman. Aboriginal women were often the only women in the remote areas drovers travelled. Some became sexual partners for brief liaisons; other relationships lasted longer and resulted in the women doing double duty as partners and stockmen.

As for their abilities with stock, author Herbert Barker detailed the skills of one of the Aboriginal women (whom he refers to as gins) he encountered in his book *Droving Days*:

> The best work on horseback that I ever saw a gin do was cutting out cattle on a camp at Ethel Creek, a big cattle station at the head of the Fortescue River. There were about 500 cattle on the camp, and the head stockman and a gin, Bullockie by name, began cutting out. She could not have done better, showing plenty of headwork when bringing them to the outside and steering them to the nearest man on the face of the camp, opening their ranks just right for the face man to dive in and cut off the wanted one while she hunted the others back to the mob. It was most interesting to watch but rather spoilt by an odd man from the back of the camp chipping in to do a bit of cutting out himself. This is fatal, and I heard Bullockie on another occasion get cross with a boy for doing it. He was her son.

Mary Durack in *Kings in Grass Castles* quoted her father's diary from the 1890s with regard to Wave Hill:

> Sunday on one of the most isolated stations in Australia. The musterers, Sam Kelly, Horace Bennison, three blk. boys, five gins. What a transformation! The many-coloured dresses of the women have now given place to shirts, moleskin pants and stockwhips slung across their shoulders. They are not now easily to be distinguished from the sterner sex but for their fuller posterior curves …

Mary added:

> From this time until a Native Administration Act put a stop to the employment of women in the cattle camps was probably the heyday of the black women who never before or since enjoyed such status and sense of importance. Small-boned and timid-seeming, they soon proved themselves to have more endurance and intelligence than their men in the cattle game. They loved the life of the stock camps, the thrill of riding the plains where they had dug for yams and scratched for lizards and if they served other ends than mustering and holding cattle little evil was prevented by confining them to the boredom of the homestead wurlies on the creek banks.

> (Durack, M., *Kings in Grass Castles*, Constable, London, 1959, p.355)

Despite the odds against them, a select few women managed to build reputations as drovers and stockmen. One of the earliest was Hannah Glennon. She was born at Toowoomba on 18 July 1872, the last of eight children of Irish emigrants John Glennon and Catherine Pickham. John had worked as a bullock teamster before settling on a smallholding in the Westbrook district, south-west of Toowoomba.

A year after Hannah was born, her father started to go blind, which threw much of the work of running the property onto her mother and an older brother, Bill. In May 1874, John Glennon died. Soon after, Hannah's mother married a man named Daniel Ryan. Bill eventually left home and went to work as a stockman on stations in western Queensland. He soon earned a reputation as an excellent rider and Hannah, fifteen years younger, had a ready-made role model whenever he returned to the farm. Twice a year, Bill returned home with a small mob of unbroken horses. Under his tutelage, Hannah became an expert rider and horse breaker.

In 1885, when Hannah was just thirteen, her stepfather died, and the weight of running the farm fell upon Hannah and her mother. Only a year later, however, her mother also died. Hannah and Bill tried to keep the farm going but the work and returns just weren't there. The property was sold and Bill went back to work as a stockman out west. Hannah was too young to follow and was taken in by relatives of her stepfather. Her new family taught her the finer points of domestic life but her passion remained with horse work.

Her skills impressed William Beit, the son of a local grazier, who witnessed her horsemanship when she was still a teenager. In 1946, writing under the pen name Pierie Remot in the *North Queensland Register*, Beit recalled:

> One day in the home yard, I saw her ride in breeches, boots and spurs. The horse was a low-set, short-backed, strong-boned animal, said to have been sent from the Lockyer District just to try Hannah out. He had already thrown the best riders on the Lockyer, and Black Peter Rouse from the Logan. She saddled him in the ring yard. Getting the reins righted, Hannah took a lug hold on him and landed on his back like a fly and rammed the spurs into him. The outlaw held his wind, giving seven or eight vicious bucks, and pulling to get his wind, he made two more desperate attempts to unseat his rider. It was a picture to see Hannah sitting calmly and unconcerned, like a 'Swell' in his Rolls Royce.

Bill was killed in a riding accident on a western Queensland station in 1888. Hannah was devastated by the loss of her closest brother, but at the age of sixteen she thought she was ready to strike out on her own. She may not have had much choice, as she'd reached an age where she could reasonably be expected to go out to work. By then Hannah had developed into a striking-looking young woman – tall and slender, with a mane of bright red hair.

In 1898 she was thought to be working on Mount Devlin Station, east of Cloncurry in the Hughenden area. In that year Michael Durack, son of Patrick Durack who had established Thylungra Station on Cooper Creek and several stations in Western Australia, was a passenger in a Cobb and Co. coach travelling from Cloncurry to Hughenden. As the coach neared Hughenden a woman riding a large black stallion flagged it down. She and her horse were so striking that Durack recorded the details in his diary:

> One person encountered on my journey is worthy of special comment – a woman, tall, gaunt-looking and with bright red hair, who helped us rummage for her mail before riding away.

When Durack made enquiries about her, the locals told him the woman's name was Red Jack. Her stallion was called Mephistopheles. A legendary if enigmatic figure, she was a bit of a loner.

Hannah continued working as a stockwoman in central Queensland, the Gulf Country and the Atherton Tableland for the next four years. She was still in the area in 1904, probably mustering cattle on Chillagoe Station, when she suffered a fall from her horse. Alive but seriously injured, an attempt was made to transport Hannah to Mareeba Hospital, some 100 kilometres away. Part of the journey may have been by rail but it was to no avail. Hannah died on 21 December 1904, aged only thirty-two. She was buried in Mareeba but her grave can no longer be located.

Yet Hannah's memory has endured, and she has become an obscure but legendary figure in the outback. Unfortunately, like so many women (and men) before her, there is precious little detail of a life spent on horseback behind cattle far from journals of record. Nevertheless, the great chronicler of outback life, the late Marie Mahood, said this of Hannah:

> She was only 32 but her name was legendary across North Queensland because she had dared the social conventions to do what she did best, to work in a man's world, where she was apparently accepted without question because of her extraordinary skill.

Much more is known about the woman who is credited with being the first female boss drover in the country. Edna Zigenbine belonged to the generations of outback children born and raised behind mobs of livestock. She was born at Thargomindah, near the Queensland–New South Wales border 1000 kilometres west of Brisbane, on 10 October 1926, the fifth of eight children of boss drover Harry Zigenbine and his wife, Ruby.

As she moved from camp to camp, spelling on the edge of towns like Marree, Tennant Creek and Camooweal, Edna's mother struggled to raise her kids and teach them the basics of schooling by correspondence. In later years, Edna looked back at what her mother went through and realised how hard it must have been for her. Every child was born in a different place. The youngest child, Mavis, was born under a tree at the Butru railway siding, near Dajarra.

The older children were supposed to ride to school in Dajarra, but as Edna later told the President of the Drover's Camp Association, Liz Flood, 'Of course we didn't go. We used to go riding all day.'

As soon as they were old enough, Edna and her siblings were in the saddle, working for their father round the clock, droving cattle and standing night watches. At a time when many outback men regarded their wives and children as a source of free labour, the average age that many youngsters left school and went to work was thirteen or fourteen. In the case of the Zigenbine kids, it was probably much earlier. Edna may have been exploited by her father but she loved the life, and in later years said she 'wouldn't change it for quids'.

Despite the attractions, in the mid-1940s Edna and her younger sister Mavis left droving and went to work as ward maids at the Tennant Creek Hospital. However, in 1950, her father found himself short-handed when R.M. Williams asked him to help take a mob of bullocks from Bedford Downs down the Murranji and on to Queensland after another drover pulled out. At the time Harry was at Hidden Valley Station, just north of the Murranji Track, and he called on his daughter to help him out.

Edna quit her job and at the age of twenty-three got back in the saddle, along with her brothers Jack and Andy. R.M. and stockman Jackie Cadell flew up from Adelaide. They rendezvoused at No. 12 Bore on the Murranji and brought the cattle through to Newcastle Waters.

Due to his business interests, R.M. had to leave them there. The party continued on to the Ranken River, where the cattle had to go through a dip to exterminate ticks before they crossed the border into Queensland. The tick inspector used too much arsenic and the cattle suffered severe burns. Harry sent R.M. a telegram along the lines of: 'Cattle burnt in dip. Expect to lose the lot. Come at once.' R.M. replied, 'Can't come. Sending nurse.' R.M. wasn't sure whether Harry would enjoy the humour, but most of the cattle were saved.

Edna continued droving with her father. On a subsequent trip he became so ill he had to pull out, leaving Edna and her younger brother Andy with a mob of cattle still to be delivered. The 23-year-old Edna continued on with her brother, who was the camp cook, three Aboriginal stockmen and one white stockman. At Crow's Nest Bore some of the cattle came down with pleuro but Edna couldn't give them a break to recover because there wasn't enough feed in the area. A stock inspector shot seventy head but declared the rest immune. At Elliott, on the Stuart Highway, one of the Aboriginal stockmen pulled out. Edna's droving team was down to five as they crossed the Barkly Tableland.

At Lake Nash, near the Queensland border, the white stockman pulled out as well. Fortunately, it was a relatively easy ride down the Georgina to Dajarra but it meant night watches of three hours instead of two for the reduced staff of four. And, of course, everyone droved the cattle right through the day. At Dajarra, 1600 head were loaded. There'd been no rushes. The cattle had been quiet the entire trip.

In droving, reputation is everything. Boss drovers who lose or mistreat cattle soon find no one will trust them with their stock. It was a testament to Edna's ability when, at the beginning of the next droving season, she was given another mob to drove, from Banka Banka Station 100 kilometres north of Tennant Creek. Says Marie Mahood:

Pam Gobbert, head stockwoman of the stud camp, Alexandria Station, 2011, responsible for much of the station's breeding program.
(Evan McHugh)

Ashley (left) and Kate Gray processing calves on Wave Hill Station, in 2011. On Wave Hill equal opportunity means women are treated exactly the same as men.
(Evan McHugh)

Opposite: Stockman Ronald Kerr with his seventeen-year-old wife Mavis and baby Johnny, c.1955.
(Jeff Carter, National Library, an9070713)

It was said of Edna that she was as good as any man with bullocks and steers and better with cows or a mixed mob. If a cow calved on the trip, Edna would pick up the newborn calf and ride with it to the cook's wagon. When they stopped for the night she would mother-up the cows and their calves and the next day the calves would get a ride on the wagon until they were strong enough to walk the daily distances with their mothers. With these mobs Edna often delivered more cattle than she had started out with. From the Kimberleys to Queensland Edna was first-choice drover for station owners who wanted to shift a mob which included cows.

In later years many of Edna's friends and acquaintances pointed out that she couldn't abide cruelty to animals. They laughingly said she would always feed her horses before she fed them. Yet she also displayed qualities that had been learned from a lifetime around stock, and the owners of stock valued such qualities. Another woman, M.M. Bennett, explained why in a book about her father, *Christison of Lammermoor*:

> Quietly handled docile animals, habituated to the routine of being herded by day and watched by night, travel well and put on condition. It is the carefully bred, quietly handled bullock that fetches the highest price. Unfortunately, people are never merciful because it pays, but only if they are mercifully inclined, so men who ought to know better will gallop after cattle, knocking them about, terrifying them and making them wild – scrubbers only fit to be shot and left – and then boast of it to people as stupid as themselves.

It is worth noting that Edna was given her father's droving plant over any of her brothers. The fact that a physically slight, relatively young woman was shouldering the responsibilities and pressures of a boss drover attracted widespread attention and publicity.

Throughout the 1950s Edna continued droving with her father's plant. She was eventually joined by John Jessop, whom she married in the early 1950s. In 1954 she gave birth to her only son, also named John, and the small family continued on the road, as Edna's parents had done before her. In 1960, Edna and John separated. The writing was on the wall for droving and Edna headed for Mount Isa, where her lack of education didn't stop her getting a job with the council as a pound keeper, responsible for tending to stray stock, particularly horses. Being settled in one place meant she had a chance to provide her young son with a more stable life than she had known.

Edna kept her own horse in the backyard of her house, and the verandas of her house resembled those of a station homestead – piled with saddles, bridles and swags. Her home became a handy stop for passing stockmen, young ringers or old friends from her droving days.

Long after she stopped droving and even after she retired, Edna continued to attract considerable interest and publicity. However, Edna's neighbour and friend Liz Flood pointed out that towards the end of Edna's life, when people were writing stories saying she was a legend and a national icon, she couldn't help feeling the words and notoriety weren't worth much as she struggled from pension to pension.

Nevertheless, she never lost her generous spirit. Says Liz: 'You could always go to Edna's place. If you didn't have a bed, the door was always open, and many a night she'd have five or six blokes staying there.'

Marie Mahood noted the understated praise that the old drovers gave her:

Edna's name is recognised by all and praise conceded by those who know themselves just how difficult the life of a boss drover could be. They are not given to extravagant praise, those old-timers. The top performers may rate only the comment, 'He was a good man on the job.' That's what they say about Edna. 'She was a good man on the job!'

Women are still working with stock, perhaps more than ever. While researching *The Drovers* book, I came across a mob of cattle being droved down the long paddock just outside Winton. Two people were behind the mob as it slowly fed along towards their dinner camp. One was a man. The other was a woman.

On Brunette Downs Station, on the Barkly Tableland, manager Henry Burke maintained in an interview in 2011 that more women were applying to work as stockmen than males.

'There seems to be a lot more girls putting their hands up at the moment,' he said. 'I think it's just working with the animals. Horses and cattle and that sort of stuff appeal to them. It's a self-test for some young people as well. They learn a lot of skills, there's a huge number of skills in being a competent cattle-stock person. If you take all those things into consideration, with machinery and vehicles and fencing and plants and animal husbandry and everything to go with it, there's a lot of skill.'

Just across from the workshops on Brunette Downs, a group of young jackaroos and jillaroos were learning how to shoe horses. The horses had been running at the ABC races the day before and were about to head back to the stock camps. I poked around, taking photographs, until a tall, weathered-looking woman asked if there was anything she could help me with.

Joy McNeven turned out to be head stockwoman in the stud camp. She was initially a little gruff, but when she found out I was researching a book, she was happy to explain things. She had been supervising the shoeing, one of the skills first-year jackaroos and jillaroos must learn.

'Most already know what to do, but if they don't they get taught,' she said. 'First years might not have a clue. They may not do the best job you'll ever see and the shoes won't stay on for six weeks, but at least they're on. They're learning and they get better.'

Joy grew up on stations around Cloncurry, which, as she pointed out to me, has trees and hills, features that are noticeably lacking out on the Barkly. She'd recently gone to Daly Waters, which has escarpment country. 'That was pretty exciting,' she said.

Joy had come up through the ranks. She'd run the stud camp for some time but recently stepped up to become head stockwoman, involved in the breeding program, in particular improving fertility.

'That's pretty well where I was hoping to be,' she said. 'My partner is a head stockman here as well.'

Over at the Brunette Downs racetrack I also met jillaroo Annabel Guthrie, a fresh-faced sun-burnished young woman in her early twenties. She was raised on a sheep and cropping property at Donald in Victoria. She had completed a four-year degree in exercise science and rehab before taking a year to head outback to get her hands dirty among the livestock.

'I wanted to go to Kununurra but Dad's best mate breeds cattle for AA [Australian Agricultural Company] and knows [manager] Henry [Burke] and [his wife] Bernadette. I applied and got the job within a month. I found out I'd got it two days before Christmas. I started in the last week of February, as a jillaroo. I'm in the commercial stock camp. There's a head stockman, two jillaroos and five jacks. We muster on horse or bike, depending on how rough the country is. We'll do yard work for two days with weaners, branding calves. You get to do everything, even preg-testing. Then there's a day or two trucking. Then we do it all again.'

She found the work challenging and at times frustrating. Not coming from a cattle background meant she sometimes struggled with knowing what to do. However, the job had plenty of satisfaction.

'It's a good feeling when you finish a big day's walk. You see the bore and the cattle arriving. After a big day you sit around the campfire and talk about being rolled by a cow or whatever. Half the days you can be hating your life, doubting yourself, but you get there. You get a sense of achievement, say, walking a mob 22 kilometres.'

The company is an equal-opportunity employer, and there is no discrimination when it comes to work.

'We do exactly the same as the boys,' Annabel said. 'In the yards you do the same. Mechanically, I'm probably not as good, but I can do more with horses.'

Jillaroo Annabel Guthrie on Brunette Downs, Northern Territory, 2011.
(Evan McHugh)

One of things she enjoyed most about Brunette was the social life.

'You make a lot of friendships in the stock camp,' she said. 'I'm very lucky we're a good group, close as friends. The people are down to earth, connected. Henry's funny. He's hardly ever around but he's great with names and faces. Always good for a laugh. Bern [Henry's wife Bernadette] is just so good, especially with us girls. She's a second mum. You can go to her with any problem, but she can be very direct.'

After four months at Brunette, Annabel was keen to do another year in the Territory. She also wanted to do more study, either in teaching or agriculture. One thing was certain; it wouldn't be at a city university.

'I've got no desire to go to the big smoke,' she said. 'It'll be a rural uni and a rural job.'

A couple of days later, I met another head stockwoman. Over in the main office at Alexandria Downs, on the Barkly Tableland, Pam Gobbert was grappling with a malfunctioning computer. I actually knew how to fix it, in return for which she took a few minutes to talk about what she did. At twenty-six, she had been working with NAPCO, which has owned Alexandria Station for more than a century, for seven years.

Pam grew up at Mitchell in central Queensland on what had been a sheep property but was now running cattle. After finishing agricultural college in 2004, she started out as a jillaroo, then became a leading hand and was now head stockwoman for the stud operation.

'I work solo but the camps help with the yard work,' she said. 'A lot of the work is entering data into the computer. There are 750 top stud cows, 2000 bull breeders, 1500 stud-bull growers, and 1500 heifer growers ready to join. I've also been doing things on the composite [breeding] side and I'm in charge of the station's stallion.'

Pam said that much of the work she was doing wasn't being done anywhere else.

'There's a lot of forward thinking,' she said. 'We do estimated breeding values, tail-hair sampling, feedlot trials, progeny testing. I've learnt on the job and done training courses.'

Pam has seen the results of NAPCO's innovative composite breeding program (which aims to produce better quality cattle suited to the Barkly Tablelands environment) literally in the flesh. 'Composite breeding means cattle are more uniform and uniformly better. And that's the whole 60 000 on the property, not just one herd. Their temperament is better. At Alexandria the focus is on fertility, adaptability and temperament.'

Pam believed the reason she'd stayed and advanced was the quality of the company she was working for. 'They have a good attitude towards young people,' she said. 'If you prove you can do the job and know what you're doing, they listen.'

Had she experienced any discrimination? Her answer hinted at what's now possible for a capable woman who's good at her job.

'I have encountered a bit of chauvinism, but I'm still here and they're not.'

THE STOCKMAN'S WIFE

When we settled down at this spot it was a rough life for the hardiest man to encounter, yet my wife was not deterred from facing it, although she never had experienced what is called country life before. The cheerful countenance with which she toiled through the drudgery of domestic occupations was what often spurred me on to greater exertion, that I might be able to build a better covering for her and my children than a bark gunya. To us bushmen these are the ministering angels to all our comforts; and you will agree with me when you visit a station where they are not. To a bachelor a bush life is a solitary life at best; and his mental culture does not improve in the way of refinement during a long absence from the society of his equals, as the case must necessarily be in a thinly peopled wilderness.

Samuel Mossman & Thomas Bannister, *Australia Visited, and Revisited*

LIVING HERITAGE

King's Messengers

The Queenslander

ILLUSTRATED WEEKLY

6d

Registered at the G.P.O., Brisbane, for transmission by post as a newspaper. For rates see page 3.

February 25, 1937

JAMES WIENEKE

Features The Murdered Man's Story — The Old Focus at Home — Happy Mr. Hardy

While the glory days of droving passed in the mid-1960s with the coming of the 'beef roads' and mechanised transport, the drovers from that previous era (and more modern times) are still around and can still recall their exploits as they took cattle from one side of the country to the other. Their heritage is preserved at the Drovers Camp at Camooweal, which was once a crossroads of the country's great stock routes.

Every year the drovers gather for an annual festival where they can catch up with mates and yarn about the old days. In 2009 I was able to interview many of them about their experiences. If there was one theme that ran through their conversations, it was that the romantic portrayal of their lives was a long way from reality.

'You get about five hours sleep a night,' Dave Allworth told me. 'The boss drover probably only gets about four hours a night for three months. The tucker's pretty basic. You can sit back after you've had dinner and you can go to sleep just like that. You get used to gettin' by on four or five hours sleep, but your body's not used to it. Just like that. It's amazing.'

Camped out beneath the starlit skies, the tree-tops overhead,
A saddle for a pillow, and a blanket for a bed,
'Twas pleasant, mate, to listen to the soughing of the breeze,
And learn the lilting lullabies which stirred the mulga trees.

Harry 'Breaker' Morant, 'Since the Country Carried Sheep'

Dave started life in New South Wales but he was determined to work in the frontier world of the Northern Territory. In 1954, when he was sixteen, the Vesteys company sent him to one of its stations, Morestone in Queensland, to learn how to be a stockman.

'You mightn't like it at the time,' he said of the experience, 'but if you get onto a property where there are hard men who know what they're about – good cattlemen, good horsemen – then they'll teach you. The manager threatened to give me a floggin' one day but that's the closest I ever got.

'They taught me how to shoe, pack horses, ride rough horses. They'd put me on a horse and say, "He's a young horse, you can both learn together."'

Dave did his time as a stockman on stations, in his case in the Northern Territory, before putting a droving plant together. He ended up droving on the Murranji and Barkly stock routes in the final years that those routes were used.

For many drovers, the different stock routes they droved largely influenced their experiences. As Bob Savage recalled:

The best trip was down the Georgina. We took bullocks across the Ranken Plain. It was downs country the whole way. There wasn't a tree anywhere. We had a competition once to try and find a leaf out there. There were windmills every 10 miles [16 kilometres]. You'd start out in the morning and you'd soon see the top of the next windmill, so you could already see where your night camp would be. And the cattle were a good mob. Bullocks. They'd stride out, 'cause you were only pushing them towards water. The only delays were when we'd stop to give 'em a good drink, because 1500 cattle take a lot of watering.

The worst trip was over to Halls Creek. On the track from Halls Creek to Broome a lot of drovers had bad smashes. I was 20 miles this side of Broome and the scorpions were crawling all over the cattle. They were this big. [He holds his hands about 30 centimetres apart.] I actually saw this scorpion on the face of one of the cattle that was lying down. It pulled back and the next thing you know it was up and away.

I had a smash there and the other drovers were going, 'You're not laughing now.'

And I said, 'I never laughed.'

I had plenty of rushes. I had one where the cattle rushed and wouldn't stop. We headed 'em and kept 'em on the stock route but they kept on rushing. They'd go along at a trot for a bit and then they'd gallop again. We just had to keep 'em going. It was pitch dark. By the end of it we were praying for the sunrise. Then they got out on the feed and pulled up.

Charlie Rayment was one drover I'd met several times while living in Birdsville. Now in his eighties, Charlie is quietly spoken – and sharp as a hawk. He still competes in bronco branding, the traditional western Queensland and Northern Territory method for branding calves. And he's pretty good at it.

Charlie was raised in 'Waltzing Matilda' country around Winton, where he eventually acquired his own property and still resides today. Among many experiences in a very full life, the consummate horseman enlisted in World War II, only to find himself in the Navy. He was serving aboard the heavy cruiser HMAS *Australia* when it was attacked and hit by kamikaze planes on six separate occasions.

He's another of the old-school drovers who doesn't mind taking the time to answer questions. Nevertheless, I was in such awe of the man that it was daunting to approach him. Typically, he knew what I was up to and came over for a bit of a yarn.

I've been droving over different areas of Queensland, around Clermont and the Belyando River Country, Longreach and Winton, the Channel Country,

Diamantina and Georgina River routes, and the country in between. A little in the Territory from Alroy Station and a little in the top of South Australia.

My first complete three-week trip, as a fourteen-year-old, was with Brighton Downs fats to Winton. The boss was a half-caste gentleman, Johnny Williams. After World War II, I worked for several boss drovers. Then in 1950 I had my own packhorse plant, mainly doing trips from the Georgina country to railheads at Quilpie, Yaraka and Winton.

My longest trip was with 1500 Territory store bullocks down to the railhead at Trangie, New South Wales. It turned out to be a 26-week trip. I think it was 1952. I had four men and myself and sixty head of plant horses. It was an easy trip with plenty of feed and water.

We walked 'em down from Camooweal, down the gutter there [the Georgina River] and over to Dajarra. Then we went down, following the rivers and the soft country – crossed the Barcoo then on to the Paroo, followed it down, then crossed the watershed to the Warrego at Cunnamulla. Followed it down then crossed over some deserty country to the Darling, which was in flood, and crossed the cattle over the old bridge at North Bourke.

We 'let go' a lot once we crossed the Queensland border, at the Barringun Gate. 'Letting go' means 'not watching'. They were broke-in bullocks by then, so we'd put them on camp at dark, settle them down and camp behind them. They would stay on camp most of the night, then towards morning they'd get up and stretch, then feed off the way we were going. You never 'let go' if they were thirsty or hungry. Next morning it was just a case of pushing them together, perhaps giving them a count, and you were already several miles along the way.

There's some bad country east of Bourke so we followed the Darling up on the east side to where the Bogan comes in, then followed it up through Nyngan and on to Trangie. I got to Trangie and them wheat stacks was gettin' higher and higher and closer together, and the fences were everywhere and I thought, 'That'll do me. Trangie was far enough.' The bullocks ended up at Hay on the Murrumbidgee, while the long trip back with the horse plant was ahead of us. No road-trains then.

That's the thing about the stock routes. They follow the softer country – the waters and the rivers – and avoid the stony ground. You wouldn't take cattle over the ranges to somewhere like Mackay if you didn't have to. The roads these days stick to the ridges. Very few follow the stock routes, the softer country. So you get these people hauling their caravans saying they've been over here and over there but they haven't really seen the country. All they've seen is the bitumen. Their rigs are too heavy to get in and see what the country is really like.

Horse drover on the Barkly Tableland in the Northern Territory, c.1960. He was taking 160 horses from Larrimah in the Northern Territory to Biloela in Queensland, about 2500 kilometres, with his horse, rifle, minimal pack and old dog.

(Robin Smith, John Oxley Library, State Library of Queensland, 196405)

Daryl Horkings was born in Warragul, Victoria, in 1948. His family moved to Tocumwal in New South Wales soon after, and the droving bug bit while he was still at school.

'As kids we'd be allowed to watch the drovers go past,' he remembered. 'They were my heroes. That's what I was gonna do when I grew up.'

After leaving school he went straight to work as a stockman with other drovers. Then he spent a few years breaking in horses before returning to the Riverina in 1973 to take up work as a drover for himself, based in Deniliquin.

'I did a lot of drovin' around that Riverina country – through the '70s and '80s. The long paddock, we were out feeding. We were never walking cattle or sheep from A to B. Wherever feed was we'd get 'em out there to get them a bellyful.'

Deniliquin in the 1970s and 1980s was a huge store-sheep (sheep destined to be fattened for meat) sale centre. Every fortnight 70 000 to 90 000 sheep would pass through the saleyards. The sheep came from as far away as Queensland, but often the trucks dropped the stock with a drover about a month's walk, around 160 kilometres, from the saleyards. Daryl recalled:

> They'd put a lot of dollop on them in those four weeks on the road. It would depend on what the [stock] routes were like. If you come to a route and it was good, you'd just stay there. Sometimes you'd spend a week on the one route. If you were there and they were improving on the route, you'd have stayed there. You wouldn't be walkin' them miles if you didn't have to.
>
> In those days you had to do 6 mile [10 kilometres] a day with sheep and 10 mile [16 kilometres] a day with cattle. If you were walkin' they didn't charge you agistment. Then when you get a good year and there's feed everywhere you could sit on a reserve. A reserve had something like 5000 acres [2000 hectares] on it and you could sit there as long as you wanted and just pay agistment. It was cheap in those days – half a cent a day for sheep and five cents a day for cattle. They'd only let you do that when there's 5000 acres of green feed there a foot high. You could stay there a bloody month and you wouldn't see what they'd eaten. It'd be growin' faster than they could eat it. I did that with sheep and cattle, some horses.

When he could, Daryl tried not to lock his stock in yards at night. He believed they did better if they were allowed to roam free, just not too far. To keep them from wandering, he pegged dogs around them. If he was camped on a fenced stock route, he simply pegged four dogs at each end.

'They were just mongrels,' Daryl explained. 'They were just pegged there to make a noise to stop your sheep or cattle walkin' up the road, but.'

In addition, Daryl had six or seven working dogs. They were never used

as peg dogs, but were kept in camp at night and well looked after. When he droved, Daryl often did so with only the dogs to help him. At the most, there was only him and another stockman: 'The dogs did most of the work, whether it was sheep or cattle. Each dog's worth three men. If you had to employ a couple of blokes, six or seven dogs'd do the same job and all you had to do was feed them. If you had a mob of sheep there was always enough killers in there for your tucker box and your dogs – old scraggers you'd get for killers. You'd pick old sheep up walking along the road – well they'd be dog tucker.'

A truck and caravan were the droving plant. Most of the time the caravan was only used to sleep. Daryl cooked inside if it was raining; otherwise he cooked at his campfire because he didn't have to clean up. 'You just peel your spuds and toss the peels in the fire,' he said.

Daryl also recalled that the traditional animosity towards drovers from local property owners hadn't diminished.

'Some of them cockies used to grow a lot of rice around that Deni area and they weren't supposed to do it but they'd drain their rice water out onto the stock route and these cockies'd be watchin' this feed growing and think, "Oh, I'll put me cattle out there and eat that down." And you'd come along with 5000 sheep and it'd be gone in a day. They used to hate us.'

Like all good drovers, Daryl always finished a drove with the same number of stock he started with. If he was ever short when he did a count he'd backtrack and usually find the missing stock in a cockie's paddock.

Daryl reckoned droving was a mixed bag: 'Drovin' down that Riverina it was either the worst job you could have or the best job and there was no in-between. The worst of it – cold winter, freezing cold weather, bloody big frosts, drought time, no feed and not much water. And you'd be pushin' and pushin' and pushin' to do your 6 mile. About four o'clock you're bloody worn out. It's gonna be dark in an hour's time, the yards you're pokin' at are still a mile away up the road and the frost is startin' to come in. You're buggered and your dogs are buggered from pushin' these wet sheep along the road. And you've gotta get there before it gets dark because a lot of times in that country when it's gonna be frost there's also fog, thick fog. You had to be locked up before dark; otherwise you'd lose 'em in the bloody fog.'

And the good times?

'There was one year, '81; I had a mob of sheep, an old rodeo mate, Bonny Young, had cattle, and we just boxed 'em together. We come along together. We spent a fortnight on the one reserve. Just sit round the fire drinkin' tea. There was nothin' else to do. The owner'd come out and say, 'Gee, you're doin' a good job,' and we'd done nothin' but sit by the fire. The other extreme you'd battle and work trying to get 'em a feed and the owner'd come out and

Stockman fitting purpose-made boots to his cattle-dog, Adavale District, Queensland, c.1900–1910. In northern regions of Australia burrs and hard stony ground could soon damage the pads of a dog's feet. Accordingly, some stockmen used their dogs sparingly, to save them for when they were most needed.
(John Oxley Library, State Library of Queensland, 34059)

A young stockman from Brunette Downs cattle station inspects a 6-foot python he caught swimming in the floodwaters while evacuating over 4000 head of Santa Gertrudis to higher ground, 1974.
(Ern McQuillan, 1926-, National Library of Australia, vn3585659-s25)

say, 'Gee, they're not doing too good, are they?' Because they've lost weight since he saw 'em two days ago.'

Daryl reflected the attitudes of many drovers when he summed up his thoughts: 'I look back at those years I spent droving as the best of my life. Freedom. Total freedom. I suppose you're out on the road travelling like a bloody gypsy – no worries and no cares. Even when I describe those hard days they were still [about] freedom. That's what I like about 'em.'

Stumpy Adams is one of those typical outback blokes who are a little reticent on first meeting, but when he warms to you he'll yarn all day and night. He's worked at everything from stockman to stock inspector, drover to camp cook. And no, he's not real tall.

Stumpy only did one droving trip, across the Ranken Plains, west of Camooweal on the Queensland–Northern Territory border. For him, a typical day involved waking before dawn, rolling his swag, having a quick breakfast then getting going. The stockmen would poke the cattle along until lunch, when they always had a camp. Someone watched the cattle while everyone else had an hour's break.

'We just lay under a tree,' Stumpy recalled, 'put your riding boot under your head and sleep like that for an hour. Then stand up and say, "Righto, let's get goin'."'

After 'poking the cattle off camp', they let them feed all afternoon. As other drovers have noted, well-fed and watered cattle camped better at night than those that were hungry or thirsty.

'Spider and me'd be bringin' the cattle up close and [boss drover] Charlie'd be yellin' out, "Keep them cattle back." You know, keep 'em feedin' up. You don't want to get 'em too early on camp. You want 'em comin' on camp just as the sun's goin' down.'

At night, Stumpy did the midnight to two o'clock watch. As he rode around the mob, its habits soon became clear. Some were camped near the fire, some preferred to sleep a bit further away. The odd one would be trying to walk off. As he'd been taught to do, he sang to the cattle or recited poetry, anything to make a continuous noise so the cattle knew he was there and wouldn't be startled by any sudden noise he made.

'I tried to sing everything,' he said. 'If Van Gogh could've heard me, he'd've cut off his other ear.'

Stumpy reckoned droving was one of the best experiences he'd ever had. 'There's nothin' better than sittin' on a horse pokin' around looking at the birds and the country,' he said. 'After that I always used to say to young fellas, if you want to learn about cattle you want to go droving. Best way you can ever learn is looking after cattle. Watching cattle, learnin' about cattle, how they act. Everything's different. The horses are different. It teaches you to be neat and tidy. Livin' in the bush is just like, you've gotta know where everything is in the dark. I was never in a packhorse camp thing, but those fellas could pack up in the dark and have the horses ready on camp and the light'd be comin' through the trees and they'd be away.'

In January 2009, years of drought in western Queensland came to an end in spectacular fashion with a rain event that sent an enormous wave of flood-water rolling down the channels of the Georgina and Diamantina rivers.

For many of the stations in the area, the rains came after they had been forced to destock. Now, with prodigious amounts of feed springing up, they didn't have the cattle available to take advantage of the boom times.

The problem for many stations was that it was prohibitively expensive to buy store cattle and truck them in to fatten on the abundant verdure. The cost of fuel was too high. And the days of droving cattle in to fatten in the Channel Country had long since passed. Or had they?

When Lake Nash Station wanted to restock, it was never going to be a small operation. Early in 2009 the owners decided they wanted 6000 breeder heifers. That's a lot of cattle in any day and age, and getting them to Lake Nash from central Queensland, 1300 kilometres away, presented quite a challenge. Trucking them was out of the question. It was decided to drove them.

The station owners turned to one of the few drovers left in the business in Queensland, Bill Prow. Bill was still taking a couple of mobs a year from stations out west and knew the stock routes well. By June he was on the road with the lead mob of 2000 heifers, travelling from Tambo through Winton, across to Boulia then up the Georgina. Behind him were two more mobs of between 1500 and 2000 head, one with a young drover named Nathan Cooper, the other with drover Peter Little.

The trip took three months, travelling at an easy pace so the cattle would put on condition. Along the way the cattle became accustomed to having people around them all day, which would make them easy to handle by the time they reached the station. The other benefit of droving was that the cost compared favourably with trucking the cattle. And it was good fresh feed all the way. Plus, for those who value such things, it kept alive skills and a way of life that many might have thought had disappeared forever. Drovers may be few in number these days, but look close enough and you'll find they're still there.

THE BIGGEST STATION

A view of life on Anna Creek in the 1970s comes from a schoolteacher who taught there for two years. Peter Caust wrote of his experiences for *The Australian Women's Weekly*. At 23 000 square kilometres, Anna Creek is the largest cattle station in the world. Peter also described conditions for stockmen on the station at the time:

> A stockman's life on Anna Creek is not all roses. It is a free and easy-going life but he must live frugally and be prepared for long hours in the saddle and weeks away from the homestead. So the camps can move anywhere on the station, the stockmen's swags are taken on a camel cart driven by the cook. It also carries all his cooking gear. Camels are particularly economical in comparison to the motor car or truck, as grass and water are found in abundance, but not so petrol and diesel fuel.
>
> The stockman's day starts at sunrise or earlier, and ends at sunset. They finish off the day with a roaring fire, stories, and a mug of hot black tea, which would warm the cockles of anyone's heart.

Peter also described the experiences of camping out on the station, waking to the sounds of corellas, galahs and crows as the sun came up over the sandhills. In spring, wildflowers put on a dazzling show of variety and abundance, filling the air with their exquisite scent.

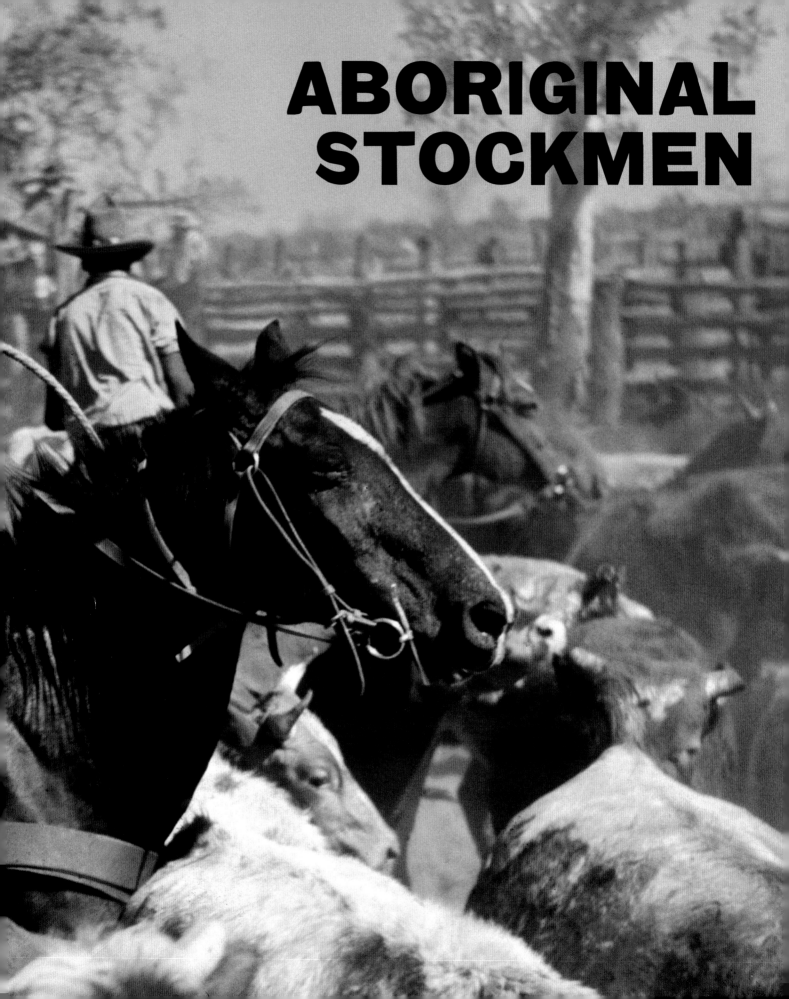

ABORIGINAL STOCKMEN

They once were warriors, defending their lands from the overlanders, squatters, stockmen and drovers. While some Aboriginal people fought with spear and shield, others sought accommodation with the newcomers. White-man rations and large docile beasts that could be herded with remarkable ease had their attractions for a people who led semi-nomadic lives pursuing often elusive game.

Men such as Jim Tyson, Nat Buchanan, John Costello, Patsy Durack, Sidney Kidman and many others recognised the potential of the original inhabitants of the land as a source of labour. Employing Aboriginal people also held the promise of security for their herds from predation. As they negotiated peacefully and recruited Aboriginal stockmen, they also discovered that mutual respect often led to relationships where the loyalty of Aboriginal stockmen went far beyond their white counterparts. Stations employing Aboriginal stockmen also gained the benefit of their intimate knowledge of their country, water sources and the changing seasons.

In the days when many stations were unfenced, when mustering was done on horseback and when stock work was done without the help of modern cattle yards, hundreds of Aboriginal people were employed in the stock camps. Many of the great outback stations in particular owed their establishment to the labour of their Indigenous stockmen. Yet as other chapters in this volume show, their contribution extended throughout the country.

Unfortunately, while working as stockmen gave Aboriginal men and women employment and a degree of status in their community, many were dependent on a sole employer for their livelihood. Instances of exploitation were all too common.

In 1936 *The Northern Standard* (published by the North Australian Workers' Union) carried a report under the title 'Wave Hill Stock Camp. Blacks Preferred to Whites. You Can Treat Them Rough'. It detailed a complaint the union had received that a head stockman on the station had refused to employ a white cook, saying, 'A blackfellow will do me; you can stick it into them.'

The report continued:

> His idea, the complainant was led to believe, is that white cooks spoil the blacks. Certainly the man in question will not spoil them with kindness, for he is a regular black nigger driver and one can hear a perpetual roaring of abuse of natives from morning to night. Whatever the man's abilities are as a stockman he certainly is not a fit and proper person to hold an Aboriginal licence or to be in charge of natives.

While the report may have involved a rogue employee, it wasn't an isolated incident. Only two years later, *The Northern Standard* carried another report that suggested the problems went deeper. Bad food was again the root of the dispute but it had got to the point that, 'There was so much trouble that stockmen, jackeroos and half-castes were about to leave in a body, but the management very shrewdly transferred the men to other stations.'

The second report further detailed labour relations at the station:

> The reputation of this station is such that many station workers refuse to take employment at any of Vesteys' stations, and it has become necessary to bring jackeroos from the south to fill the positions. These men come under agreement, but they also are dissatisfied with the conditions, and there has been nothing but trouble since the last batch arrived some weeks ago. One of the newcomers, alleged to know nothing about stock work, was placed in charge of one of the camps, but even the blackfellows rebelled at this and told the boss that 'this fella too much humbug', and said they would not work with him.

A decade later, conditions were worse, if anything. In 1949 *The Northern Standard* claimed the station employed twenty whites and 250 Aborigines, including thirty-three natives under the age of seven and another thirty-seven under the age of ten. None were being schooled. No wages were paid to any of the Aboriginal staff. Instead they were given a slice of bread and a piece of beef for every meal. The *Standard* also detailed what it described as a vicious practice:

> As there's a surplus of native labor at the station, some natives are worked for only six months and then a new team is started. This means that for six months the native has to fend for himself when he is sent 'walkabout'. In those six months a white stockman would earn about £145 and, perhaps, be able to have a holiday. But the native is forced to live on lilyroots and bandicoots. Thus he is only too pleased to get his job back on the station to obtain a bit of white man tucker. So the vicious racket continues.

The problems weren't confined to Wave Hill. In 1949 *The Northern Standard* ran an article with the headline 'No Pay – Not Enough Food or Warm Clothing'. The article was based on a letter from North Australian Workers' Union organiser George Gibbs, who had visited Lake Nash Station and maintained that in February that year Indigenous workers had threatened to walk off if they weren't paid. The threat predated the famous Wave Hill walk-off by more than fifteen years.

Eventually the then-owners, the Queensland National Pastoral Company, agreed to pay their Indigenous workers £4 per month – half in cash and half to be put into a trust account. The amount was well short of what white workers were paid. Aboriginal pumpers were only getting £1 a week while the equivalent rate for whites was more than £7. Gibbs also found one Aboriginal boundary rider who was living under basic conditions, on his own, 130 kilometres from the station. He sometimes didn't see anyone for up to six weeks at a time.

Meanwhile, the poor conditions at the notorious Wave Hill may have prompted the land's traditional owners to walk off the job around 1953. At the time, the North Australian Workers' Union didn't have a field officer for the area and hadn't been advised of the strike action. Without any outside support, the strikers were eventually starved back to work.

The goings-on at Wave Hill couldn't stay hidden forever. By the mid-1960s developments with far-reaching consequences were spreading across the outback. The construction of all-weather 'beef roads' was revolutionising the transport of stock to markets. While they may have drawn the glory days of horseback droving to an end, an unexpected by-product of the beef roads was that they made it a lot easier for people, and ideas, to travel to the stations. And the latter were far less isolated from the eyes of the world.

Civil rights activists, fired by developments in the United States, couldn't help noticing the glaring injustices in their own backyard. In March 1966 the unions and activists had a major win, when pastoral workers were awarded equal wages, regardless of their race, although stations employing Aboriginal workers were given two years to comply with the law.

Unfortunately, the push for equal rights and equal pay for Aboriginal stockmen coincided with the exact moment in history when outback stations no longer required the services of many of them. Some of the white stockmen saw the writing on the wall around 1965 and moved on to other things, many leaving the cattle industry permanently.

For Aboriginal stockmen, it wasn't so easy. In the case of Wave Hill, Nat Buchanan had managed to arrive at an accommodation (not without tensions and bloody incidents) that preserved the traditional owners' connections with their country, even as the cattle station was formed around them. However, as early as 1949, *The Northern Standard* estimated there was only enough work for half the available workforce.

Generally, stations employing traditional land owners paid them less than white stockmen, with the justification that they also provided for their families as well, and food was a component of the payment (or in some cases the only payment). While there were elements of exploitation in such relationships, there was another, unresolved issue that had managed to go

An unidentified Aboriginal
stockman leaving cattle
yards, Brunette Downs,
Northern Territory, 1974.
(National Archives of Australia, A8746,
KN19/9/74/5)

unnoticed for decades: what would happen if the relationship between the cattle station and the traditional owners broke down?

The issue finally surfaced at Wave Hill Station in 1966. In the wake of the March wages decision, the traditional owners of the Wave Hill land, who identified themselves as Gurindji, were attempting to negotiate with the station's management company, Vesteys, for better pay and conditions. Predictably, the English company was extremely reluctant to do anything, at least until 1968, when equal pay would become compulsory.

In August, the negotiations were deadlocked. The Gurindji stockmen decided they'd had enough, stopped work and left their camp at the homestead. They didn't actually leave the station because it encompassed all of their traditional Gurindji lands. To do so would have seen them trespass on land that, according to their law, still belonged to other traditional owners. So they set up camp 10 kilometres down the Victoria River from the Wave Hill homestead.

One of the most significant moments in the history of Indigenous land rights was initially described as a strike, but it soon became apparent that there was much more at stake. As time went on, it became clear that the traditional owners never wanted to work for Vesteys again. The century-old relationship between the cattle station and the Gurindji was finished.

Early in 1967 the traditional land owners relocated to a place they called Daguragu on Wattie Creek, near Wave Hill Station's boundary with Limbunya Station, a site of cultural significance and an area partly covered by a Miner's Right already held by three Gurindji people. However, they still faced the problem that in common law they had only a tenuous right to be there. Nevertheless, one of the leaders of the walk-off, Vincent Lingiari, articulated the view of the traditional owners. Frank Hardy quoted Lingiari in his book *The Unlucky Australians*: 'I bin thinkin' this bin Gurindji country. We bin here long time before them Vesteys mob.'

His assertion was that he still thought of the land as belonging to the Gurindji. All Vesteys owned was the cattle. With the benefit of hindsight, it was an incredibly powerful statement of a simple fact: his people had enjoyed unbroken tenure of the land and nothing had yet occurred to change that. No treaties, no agreements, no formal notifications and no compensation. At most there was a blanket annexure made so far away and in a foreign language that no court today would countenance it for an instant. And indeed, Vesteys only leased the land, which in common law belonged to no man. It was still Crown Land, an ethereal concept of ownership only one step removed from terra nullius.

What started as a campaign for better wages and conditions for Aboriginal stockmen on Wave Hill had become a battle for ownership of the station

itself. By April the Gurindji had articulated a plan to lease 1300 square kilometres of Wave Hill themselves, either to run their own cattle station or to remain there under the protection of a mining lease. Back at Wave Hill Station, the original Aboriginal camp was bulldozed by station management to erase evidence of the conditions they'd been complaining about.

Frank Hardy and local Aboriginal Welfare Officer Bill Jeffrey wrote a petition to the Governor-General, Lord Casey, on behalf of Vincent Lingiari, Pincher Manguari, Gerry Ngalgardji and Long-Johnny Kitgnaari, asking him to consider their 'desire to regain tenure of our tribal lands', specifically the return of the 1300 square kilometres they'd identified, on the basis that they would match the lease payments currently being paid for the land by Vesteys. With regard to compensation for Vesteys, they pointed out that the company had been more than compensated over the previous fifty years by the unpaid labour of their fathers, and meagre wages subsequently. They told the Governor-General, 'Morally the land is ours.'

The Gurindji were sent a response in June 1967, not from the Governor-General but from his secretary, who rejected the Gurindji's petition. While outlining the legal position in detail, the Governor-General's secretary avoided any reference to the moral dimension the Gurindji had raised.

However, the Gurindji weren't about to go away. Nor was the problem. The Gurindji were offered opportunities to resettle on other stations and on land reserved 'for the use and benefit of the Aborigines'. These offers were rejected because the country involved belonged to other groups of traditional owners.

While there were threats and intimidation from the Wave Hill management and local police, the Gurindji remained at Daguragu. The reason there was no concerted attempt to evict them may have been due to the civil rights firestorm it might unleash, or because the logistics of doing so were beyond the Northern Territory administration. Plus there was the vexing problem of where else the people could actually go.

Politicians, lawyers, activists and leaseholders continued to grapple with the ramifications of the Gurindji claim, which had become a touchstone for land rights activists throughout the country. Even Vesteys was coming to the realisation that some kind of concession had to be made, if only to bring the uncertainties of the situation to an end. Still, the issue dragged on.

It took a change of government, in November 1972, to change the political landscape. Gough Whitlam and the Labor Party had gone to the election with a policy to legislate in support of land rights for Aboriginal people. Even then it took three years for the claim of the Gurindji to finally be recognised. It effectively involved Vesteys surrendering its Wave Hill lease and the government reissuing two leases, one to Vesteys for Wave Hill reduced in size to 13500 square kilometres and a second lease to the Gurindji for

Michael Emms in the crow's nest of Terango yards on Adria Downs, 2012. Aboriginal stockmen are still making a major contribution to stations such as this, though in fewer numbers than days gone by. The crow's nest is used to draught cattle, such as fats, breeders, weaners and strangers, into different yards.
(Mike Bell, courtesy R.M. Williams Publishing)

Basic conditions in an Aboriginal stock camp. Frustration with wages and conditions lead to strike action and subsequent movement towards Aboriginal land rights. Date and place unknown.

(D. D. Smith Collection, Northern Territory Library, PH0323/0012)

3300 square kilometres excised from the original station. The Gurindji land included the original Wave Hill homestead, which was subsequently moved to its present location.

On 16 August 1975, Prime Minister Gough Whitlam travelled to Wave Hill to ceremonially return the land to the Gurindji. Under a makeshift awning, he poured a handful of dirt into Vincent Lingiari's hand and said, 'Vincent Lingiari, I solemnly hand to you these deeds as proof in Australian law that these lands belong to the Gurindji people, and I put into your hands part of the earth as a sign that this land will be the possession of you and your children forever.'

It was a significant moment in Australian history. The Gurindji had boasted in their petition to the Governor-General, 'We know how to work cattle better than any white man.'

The Wave Hill walk-off also marked the end of an era for Aboriginal stockmen. They were once employed in their hundreds across Australia on cattle stations and as drovers. However, the construction of beef roads greatly reduced the need for stockmen as half a dozen road trains could shift 1000 cattle in a couple of days instead of requiring half a dozen men over a period of months.

The push for equal wages, while entirely justified, had some unexpected consequences. No station could afford to employ hundreds of people at award wages. They were forced to become more efficient, particularly in staffing. Soon they were utilising helicopters, fixed-wing aircraft, motorbikes, four-wheel drives and trucks to streamline their operations. They were building modern cattle yards, with races and crushes, to make processing stock less labour-intensive.

The consequence for Aboriginal people in the outback is that many of them have gained land rights but lost their jobs. Many are now suffering the ravages of generational welfare dependency and the days when they could proudly claim to be the best of the best among stockmen have become a distant memory. Yet they can still point to a proud legacy. Many of the outback's great stations owe their genesis to the labour of Aboriginal stockmen. Without them it's doubtful those stations would exist.

VRD IN THE 1940S

A journalist from the *Sydney Morning Herald*, Barb Dwyer, visited Victoria River Downs in 1947.

> The station work is of a rough and arduous nature. Besides being good bush-men and horsemen and having an understanding of natives, the men have to be of particularly enduring fibre, for they see very little of their home-stead or quarters and virtually live out on the run in all sorts of weather.
>
> The Victoria River Downs herd is estimated at 140,000 head of cattle and the six stock camps brand about 35,000 calves annually.
>
> The five out-stations are Montejinnie, Moolooloo, Pigeon Hole, Mount Sanford and Gordon Creek. Each is in charge of a head stockman, who usu-ally has a white cook, a couple of white stockmen, ten or fifteen native stockmen, and perhaps a fencer and track rider. The work is seasonal and during the rainy season very little is done with the stock. The heavy rain turns the black soil basalt plains into quagmires, and the creeks and rivers become roaring torrents.
>
> 'The Largest Cattle Station in the World,' Barb Dwyer,
> *Sydney Morning Herald*, 7 June 1947, p. 9

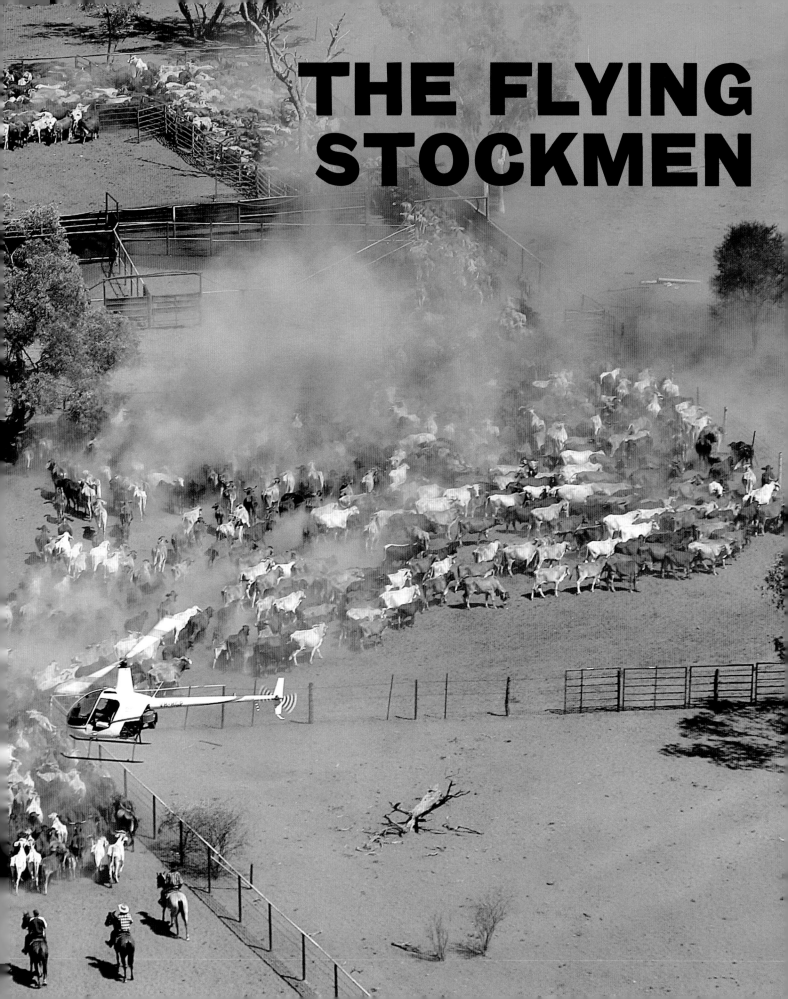

THE FLYING STOCKMEN

It was in the 1960s, when the use of light aircraft became more common for travelling the vast distances between outback stations, that a pilot (possibly Windorah's Sandy Kidd) discovered that stock would move if an aircraft passed near them. It wasn't long before fixed-wing aircraft and helicopters were being used to muster cattle and sheep in tandem with stockmen on motorbikes and horses on the ground.

Mustering pilots tend to be a young breed. The work is difficult and dangerous, the lifestyle on remote stations is challenging. However, outback aviation has the advantage of giving aspiring pilots the opportunity to get paid while adding to the flying hours needed to progress in their careers. But while a passion for flying is a pre-requisite, an ability to understand stock is also a necessity. Most mustering pilots are stockmen first and pilots second.

On 16 000-square kilometre Lake Nash Station, on the southern Barkly, chopper pilot Erin Gibson took me for a fly to muster Blenheim Paddock. Erin's Robinson R22 was parked literally at the back of his house. We couldn't take off until there was enough light, but it still meant fuelling up and doing pre-flight checks while it was dark.

Erin took one look at my clothing and offered me a heavier jacket, which I took, not being sure I'd need it to ward off the winter cold. The sun was still below the eastern horizon when we got airborne. It took about ten seconds to realise how wise Erin had been to make me bundle up. The R22's bubble did nothing to insulate us from the rotor's wind and, combined with the frosty morning air, the chill factor was breathtaking. It was half-past six and I wasn't cheered when Erin, whose job I'd envied up until a few moments earlier, told me it usually warmed up by 10 or 11 a.m. There was some hope of respite because he'd added that if it got busy while he was mustering he would drop me under a tree somewhere until things settled down.

Good luck finding a tree, I thought as we shivered our way over the wide-open grasslands to Blenheim. My fingers were barely able to move as I took photographs. The consolation was the view in the early morning light. As the sun rose, the tussocks of Mitchell grass threw long shadows.

When we got out to Blenheim, the ground crews were already in action and Erin got straight to work. We flew down the southern fence, flushing cattle out of a small belt of gidgee and heading them towards two horsemen who were gathering a mob around a waterhole, ready to walk them to the yards on the north side of the paddock.

We then flew down to the western end of Blenheim and made sweeps to push the remaining cattle east. There was no dramatic swooping and diving, the preferred result being cattle walking in the right direction, calm and steady.

Erin was safety conscious to the point of making me nervous. He did a quick check when he thought the engine was making a strange noise, then

Previous spread:
Mustering pilot Dan Clarke assists in yarding up on Carlton Hills, north of Mount Isa, Queensland, 2008. The use of aircraft and wide-wing yards has made it possible to handle immense numbers of cattle with an efficiency inconceivable in days past.
(Scott Bridle)

Mercy flight by the Royal Flying Doctor Service in western Queensland, 1969. The aircraft has just landed to render assistance to a stockman with a suspected broken leg.
(Robert Barnes, John Oxley Library, State Library of Queensland, 193541)

Mustering cattle from
the air, Lake Nash, in
cooperation with stockmen
on horseback. The chopper
is particularly effective in
rounding up stragglers.

(Evan McHugh)

mentioned a recent fiery crash in the Hunter Valley, involving the company where he'd once worked, and another in the Gulf Country.

Occasionally a beast refused to cooperate, prompting Erin to call someone on the ground to assist, if they were nearby. The cattle quickly got the message when a horseman appeared.

When the cattle were all heading in the right direction, Erin landed on a low rocky knoll in the middle of the paddock to conserve fuel. We got out and stretched our legs, then sat in the bubble of the chopper, which was warming up nicely, and not by accident. Erin had landed facing the sun. The conversation warmed at a slightly faster rate than our body temperatures.

Erin was twenty-six, raised in sheep country at Walcha, in northern New South Wales, but like a lot of farm kids he'd dreamed of the big stations.

'There's always action, road trains, helos, horses,' he said. 'Back home it was mainly horses and one bike.'

He had also wanted to fly since he was a boy. He went to work as a jackeroo as soon as he left school, then worked as an engineer with Qantas before studying to be a pilot when he got enough money together.

'I learnt to fly in Newcastle. My girlfriend at the time and I had saved a deposit to buy a house but I realised what I really wanted to do was learn to fly. We sort of went our separate ways after that.'

He got a job in the Hunter Valley, flying wine-country tourists from their farm gates to their dinner plates. Then he got a job in the outback. He got his mustering endorsement in Mount Isa and had been flying for eighteen months.

'It takes a bit of learning to heli-muster,' he said. 'It's a challenge, and good fun. A few times I've had scares. Pushing cattle out of creek beds and trees when they don't want to move requires some challenging manoeuvres. But this job is everything I'd hoped for and more.'

With his engineering skills Erin was tempted by a well-paid job in the mining region around Mount Isa but a two-week stint at Lake Nash changed all that. 'The money in the mines was better but after working here I realised I wouldn't be happy there. So I said to [station manager] George [Scott], "Is there any way we can make this permanent?" And he made it happen. He's been really good to me. Here I've got a house, all my meals and land the chopper outside the back door. The only problem is I spend a bit too much when I go into town.'

He also has a new partner, who works in Mount Isa as a teacher. When he isn't flying, there's plenty for Erin to do.

'The good thing about here is you learn how to do all sorts of things. You learn how to do the job with what you've got. You develop a better work ethic. I was a bit lazy before but now I get going.'

We talked about flying helicopters, which is clearly a skill not everyone can learn, then we got going again. Eventually the cattle were stretched in long lines across the paddock, walking into the yards.

From the chopper we could see the slowly moving threads of animals, hundreds of cows and calves spread across a plain deeply covered in grass, interspersed with man-made waterholes. It was a profoundly impressive sight, more so considering Lake Nash is one of only nine properties that cover most of the Barkly Tableland and carry between them three-quarters of a million cattle. From our lofty perch, it was hard not to look over the great sweep of country below and feel a little like a king in a grass castle.

On Wave Hill Station, chopper pilot Zeb Leslie also took me out for a fly. He was helping to muster cattle that had been turned out from the yards the previous night to graze in an adjacent paddock. Half of the 3000 cows had to be returned to the yards for the day to be preg-tested. The remaining 1500 would be tested the following day.

On the way out to the yards, Zeb gave me a tour of some of the property's features: verdant waterholes surrounded by paperbark trees, rugged flat-topped bluffs ringed by spectacular red-stone cliffs lit by the rising sun. And grass, endless seas of grass. I felt privileged to have such an unforgettable view laid before my eyes.

Zeb had been a stockman in the Victoria River region before he decided to become a chopper pilot and (as most pilots do) undertook the costly lessons at his own expense. His experience showed now as he remained at altitude, putting gentle pressure on the 3000 white Brahmans below to move them towards the yards. He coordinated with the horsemen and a motorbike rider on the ground using two-way radio. As at Lake Nash, there was no swooping or diving. Instead Zeb made slow passes along the flanks of the herd as it moved towards the yards in a growing cloud of dust. When he thought the required number of cattle had passed through the gate into the holding paddock, he alerted the dust-shrouded ground crew, who closed it, dividing the herd.

Zeb then helped push the herd that was about to be preg-tested into the yards for the day. There was a bit of action when a couple of cows tried to break from the mob, but the ground crew spurred their horses in a flash to cut them off. The bright shirts many stockmen preferred made sense amid the dust and cattle. From the air and on the ground they were highly visible. Of course, the glowing white cattle stood out like beacons.

Some stockmen wore white helmets, while others wore Akubras. Helmets

Moving Santa Gertrudis breeders off a bore in the lake country of Rockhampton Downs, Barkly Tableland, Northern Teritory, 2006. The art of aerial mustering is to put just enough pressure on stock to get them walking but not so much that they'll run, become over-heated and separate from their calves. With skilful pilots, well-handled stock will actually follow the helicopter.

(Scott Bridle)

were only compulsory for novices and the decision on when they could go without was made by the manager Greg Dakin or his head stockman.

Wave Hill used to use only helicopters for aerial mustering but recently it had reverted to fixed-wing aircraft in more open country. The station had its own plane and pilot, so rather than having him mowing lawns or raking leaves when he wasn't needed, he now went mustering.

Zeb's employer, Helimuster, was used on a contract basis. The company is based on a neighbouring property and they come over whenever they are needed.

Job done, Zeb dropped down to land near the yards. As we descended we noticed a dingo harassing a cow and young calf. If the dingo could run the cow for long enough, it would eventually become exhausted and become separated from the calf, leaving it vulnerable. Losses of calves to dingoes can be substantial on Wave Hill and the company invests a significant amount to control dog populations.

Over in the yards 1500 cows were now waiting to be preg-tested. Manager Greg Dakin was washing up in preparation for the day ahead, which was going to be anything but pleasant. His stock camp was lining up cows in a race as he pulled on a glove that reached up to his shoulder. He then slid his arm into the first beast of many, to assess whether it was in calf or not.

While watching the mustering near Crown Point Station in central Australia, I also got a chance to catch up with chopper pilot Danny Rickard.

When Danny landed, we took the doors off his R44 to make it easier to take photos, then got airborne. His task was to round up any strays that were still wandering the paddock, but he did have time to take a quick tour of the spectacular landforms around the yards and the stock camp. Soon we were exploring the stratified remnants of what was once an ancient mountain range.

He flew to the edge of a cliff then dropped into a near-vertical dive down its face. If he was trying to test my nerve, he was doing a good job. Near the rapidly approaching ground, he pulled out of the dive, cranked the machine over and raced away across the dunes in search of cattle.

'Nothing like pulling a few Gs to settle your breakfast,' I said over the intercom, trying to sound unfazed. Who was I kidding? You can't beat low-level chopper operations for a heady mixture of excitement and fear.

After executing a series of high-speed low-altitude runs with dunes looming on either side, in what felt like an outback version of the attack on the Death Star in *Star Wars*, Danny found ten beasts, including cows and calves.

Contract chopper pilot Zeb
Leslie in the air and on
the ground at Wave Hill,
2011. Fixed-wing pilot Sam
McKendry at Headingly
Station, 2011.

(Evan McHugh)

He manoeuvred them into a group then gently pressed them in the direction of the main mob.

'The trick is not too much pressure,' Danny said, echoing the softly, softly approach that was so unlike the spectacular cowboy manoeuvres usually shown on television. 'You really only need to do gentle loops.'

Gentle loops? I liked the sound of that.

On Headingly Station, young fixed-wing pilot, Sam McKendry, was a youthful-looking twenty, but had already logged 400 hours flying time as of June 2011.

'I'm a Brisbane boy,' he said, a rarity among pilots. 'I started flying when I was fifteen. I always wanted to fly. I suppose I have a different goal to most pilots, who want to get into the airlines. I'm more interested in the RFDS or corporate jets.'

Sam had been at Headingly for three months, his first job on a station.

'The choppers muster,' he explained. 'The main thing I do is inspection. I fly the fence lines to see if any cattle are hanging on the fence or in a corner. If they're hanging away from water, they'll perish. I do bore runs, check troughs and pumps.'

When he isn't flying, he pretty much does everything the other staff do: bore work, cattle work, and helping in the yards, which has its moments.

'I've been hit by a cow,' he said. 'It was my first day, in the round yard, and a big heifer got me from behind, pushed me into the rails. You've got to watch those heifers, especially the really smoky [hot-tempered] ones.'

As was the case with other properties I'd visited, Sam heard about the station through friends who'd had good experiences there. He applied for a job but initially didn't get it.

'Eventually I got a call and Steve offered me a job,' he said. 'It's a great experience. I've met people and done things I wouldn't do in a city. The flying is different – low level, a different use of the plane. It becomes a tool.'

He was also discovering a different kind of work ethic, although he may not have known it.

'I've got a hobby,' Sam told me, 'building a T-rex chopper: radio-controlled. I'm not making any progress. I'm always busy. If I'm not busy, I'm trying to sleep. I've had the chopper for two months. At home it would take me only two nights to build it.'

Aerial mustering may seem like a male domain, but not so on Commonwealth Hill Station, in South Australia. There I found one of the new breed of stockwomen, mustering pilot Andrea McHardy. The morning we met, in mid-2011, a south-westerly was blowing close to gale force, which meant aerial mustering was out of the question.

As with nearly all outback pilots, Andrea was incredibly young. The 21-year-old was raised in New Zealand on a property near Gisborne called Tangi Hau (meaning howling wind). Her father managed a 6500-hectare property that ran sheep, deer and cattle and whose biggest paddock would fit easily into the smallest on Commonwealth Hill. Despite this the property carried more sheep: 65000 on 6500 hectares compared to Commonwealth Hill's 55000 on a million hectares.

Andrea had wanted to fly since childhood.

'When I was ten I saw the movie *Pearl Harbour* and I loved it,' she said. 'I decided then that I wanted to be a pilot.'

She got her pilot's licence in November 2009 and her commercial licence in February 2010. Commonwealth Hill was her first flying job. She explained that flying on outback stations was the fastest way to get your hours up. Ultimately she would probably get a job with an airline, although she suspected there was more job satisfaction in general aviation.

'When I arrived in Australia, I went to Barry Forster at Leongatha to do my low-level endorsement,' she said. 'He's one of three people in Australia who can do that. You need to do eight to ten hours at low level but I was able to use some hours from my lessons at home. He teaches you the turns, manoeuvres and how to "bomb" the stock. You fly at 10 feet with trees coming at you, practice engine failures at low level and turns.'

Andrea heard about the job at Commonwealth Hill through a friend who was already working there. Other than doing office work to pay for her flying lessons, it was her first proper job. She applied on a Monday and was offered the job the following Wednesday.

'I arrived here on 31 January,' she said. 'I loved it. It's a true Australian experience. It's not all easy though. I like the comforts of civilisation. I was a bit shocked by the living conditions. I didn't know that there were places with wood-fired boilers for hot water. I couldn't believe how flat it was. But the people are great and mustering is awesome. I like that type of flying where you're working low. It is dangerous but it's your choice.

'I've only had one serious incident, when I was bombing sheep in 45-degree temperatures. In heat like that the plane doesn't handle the same way. I almost didn't make it out of the bomb; I almost stalled it. It was a real wake-up call and a reminder not to ask the impossible of your machine.

'Other than that I've had electrics that caused problems, a problem with the starter motor and no radio. When you don't have a radio it's surprising how well you can communicate with the ground. You can use hand signals

Fixed-wing pilot Andrea McHardy on Commonwealth Hill, 2011.

(Evan McHugh)

to show the ground crew were to go. When my radio was broken I had one Danish fellow say, "I understand you better when you're not talking." When the previous dogger had a radio problem, I flew out to find him then said, "Wave if you can hear me but can't talk back." When he did that, I then said, "Wave again if everything is okay."

Not surprisingly, Andrea finds working stock is completely different to the way she used to do it in New Zealand. When she's in the plane, she takes control of the people on the ground, directing them to the sheep.

The day we spoke she was supposed to rendezvous with the manager from Mobella outstation but he had already left the homestead when the decision was made that she couldn't go mustering. The only way to reach him was with the plane's radio when it was flying at altitude. She offered to take me for a quick flight in her Cessna 172 while she made the call.

Out at the airstrip, after doing her pre-flight checks she took off and circled the homestead so I could take some photographs. Meanwhile, her attempts to raise the manager were frustrated when the radio turned out to be malfunctioning. The radio was transmitting and receiving but Andrea couldn't hear anything through the headphones.

It turned out she'd discovered another of the hazards of flying in the outback. Mice, which were in plague proportions at the station, were the suspected cause of the problem. Andrea had been putting poison baits in the plane and they were being eaten, but one mouse seemed to have found its way to an electrical cable. As Andrea circled and tried to get some response from the radio, I tried not to think of what else the mice might have chewed.

THE WORLD'S LARGEST FLOCK

1788	The First Fleet arrived with 44 sheep
1810	33 000 sheep (mixed breeds)
1820–1850	17 million (predominantly merino but also Saxons in southern states and highlands districts)
1860–1891	108 million
1950–1970	180 million
2013	With more than 70 million sheep (with shifting emphasis to meat and live export), Australia's sheep industry comprises one fifth of the world's sheep population, while producing a third of the world's wool. Improved breeding has also seen the yield from sheep increase from an average of 1 kilo of wool in the 1820s to 5 kilos today.

(Sources: ABS and *Australians: A Historical Atlas*)

THE NEXT GENERATION

It's one of the popular myths of the outback that the days of the stockmen have long since past. In some cases authors suggest the end of the era was around the time they retired from stock work themselves. The reality is that the reins have been passed from generation to generation. Some old hands are still there, but young stockmen from Generation Y are filling the shoes of their forebears. And they're proving they've got what it takes. Contrary to the popular idea that Gen Y are slackers, when it comes to get up and go, you've got to get up pretty early to see where they went.

The life of a stockman has certainly evolved. Where once you just needed to know how to shoe a horse and ride it, and how to throw and brand a beast, now you need to repair utes, bikes and bore pumps as well. Some jobs may not have changed much, such as fencing, but mustering can involve horses, motorbikes, utility vehicles, helicopters and fixed-wing aircraft, communicating by two-way radio. On many stations, what they learn is credited towards recognised certificates in agriculture.

The attractions of stock work may be many, but it remains hard, dirty and sometimes dangerous work. Stations now find themselves in competition with mines for young staff. They're compelled to be more flexible in employment arrangements, accepting that many staff may stay only one year before moving on. They also need to provide modern amenities such as the Internet so that young staff can keep up their social networks.

On Brunette Downs Station, manager Henry Burke (interviewed in 2011) was clearly proud of his station's reputation as an employer of the younger generation. While the company that owns Brunette, AACo, runs ads in rural newspapers and magazines, many staff come as a result of referrals from past workers. Many don't stay long but Henry believed that if they went back and talked about having a good experience, some of their friends always ended up wanting to come, too. Many use the experience as a gap year, before going on to higher education.

Henry was impressed by the work ethic of Generation Y, who formed the bulk of his workforce.

'They have a go,' he said, 'particularly the type of people we get out here. I think they're getting more skilled. There's more knowledge. You can jump on the Internet if you want to Google something and say, "Well, how does this work?"'

On Lake Nash, manager George Scott felt the same way. 'These blokes can go all day,' he said. 'We used to have Barcoo rot, basically scurvy, because we saw nothing green. They can keep going because they've got the diet. And keep up the pace all through the day. They've got my admiration.'

Typical of the new breed of stockman on Brunette was Jack Henry (and Annabel Guthrie, as detailed in the chapter on stockwomen). Jack was raised on a cattle and cropping property near Warwick in south-east Queensland. He then did a Bachelor of Commerce and Business Management in agribusiness only to find he wasn't ready to start a career in accounting. While I did a double take, he explained further. He went to Canada and worked on a couple of ranches, backpacked around Europe, then came back to Australia when he was twenty-four. He was still not ready to get behind a desk and wanted to work on one of the iconic properties: Brunette, Newcastle Waters or Victoria River Downs. He applied for jobs on all three. A friend whose father worked at AACo got him a start at Brunette.

'I love it here,' he said. 'I'm a first-year jackaroo in the bullock camp out on the lakes. There are five jacks and head stockman Chris Keane, and we're often camping out and roughing it. This wet, we couldn't get the trailers out there so it was akin to the 1950s and 1960s-style stock camps. The old fellas reckon we were doing it old style, which they hadn't seen for many years. We all really embraced it. We swam in turkey's nest dams, cooked on fires.

'I thought I knew cattle but large mobs move differently, act differently. I had to relearn mustering. Dad and I could muster a mob back home, but here it takes six or seven plus a chopper, communicating by radio.'

In Jack's stock camp, most of the crew had only two years' experience or less. However, he reckoned the head stockmen were great trainers. He had also found that being so far from help made him prepare better in case things went wrong, and this made him more self-reliant.

'You'll get your orders in the morning,' he said, 'and you'll have to remember them all day, because the boss might be 30 kilometres away. You have to know when you're understanding and not understanding. And you can't say you can't do it, because you have to do it.'

Then there are the experiences you won't get anywhere else.

'You do get these "pinch yourself" moments. Like when I was on a bike pushing cattle off a bore with a plane bombing them and coming in only 2 or 3 metres above. You're riding flat-chat, you can't see anything because of the dust churned up by 1000 head, then there's the drama when the Cessna bursts through the dust, going flat-chat, then it's gone.

'And the first time you throw and tie a beast and see you're able to do it. There are moments like that.'

I was ready to sign up. However, Jack still wasn't sure about his future.

'I'm at a bit of a crossroads,' he said. 'I've applied for a bank job, with a six-month application process. That's been successful and I've been asked to start. However, Henry has been talking to me about having a future with AACo. So I'm still fifty-fifty as to which way I'll go.'

Jackaroo Jack Henry on Brunette Downs, Northern Territory, 2011.

(Evan McHugh)

'If you had to choose today,' I asked, 'would you rather sit behind a desk or sit behind a mob of cattle?'

He said that he'd take the cattle in a heartbeat, but he still had to think about the long term.

On the NAPCO-owned Alexandria Downs Station, on the Barkly, I managed to meet up with another of the 'new breed' of stockman. While road trains have been used to move stock to market since the 1960s, on the largest stations in Australia they are also used to move them from paddock to paddock. The skills required go beyond being able to drive the truck. The objective is to minimise stress and injuries to the stock as well.

Road-train driver Johnny Rankine was one of NAPCO's longest-serving employees, and a legendary figure on the Barkly. He was the grandson of the Rankine Store's original owner, George Watson, and has lived on Alexandria Downs Station since 1965, when he was sixteen.

J.R. was a keeper of many of the station's stories, some of which he told with delight. I'd been coached to ask him about ghosts, and he lit up at my question.

'There's a ghost here on the station. He used to be a boundary rider on Soudan. Someone had run a cable between two trees and when he was out galloping it chopped his head clean off. I've seen him at Number 41 gate. It was night and he came up and asked for a smoke. He just came up beside me. I said, "I don't smoke", and he went on his way. The second time I saw him was at Gidgee, when I was watching stock. I saw this bloke open a gate and let the cattle out. I thought, "*That's crazy*", and took off after them.'

J.R. had an easy manner about him, a ready smile, and an obvious pride in his work. As we talked, we sat on a pile of old tyres, down in the shed where he kept the prime mover for the station road train that he drove. His hair was grey and dishevelled, his clothes were smudged with grease and dirt, but his truck was immaculate. It looked like it had just been driven off the showroom floor, not over hundreds of kilometres of station tracks.

'A few blokes have seen that ghost,' he continued. 'Usually it happens when they're driving trucks and opening gates. He asks for a smoke. You know that feeling when your hair goes on end? He just gets up alongside, on your side when you're not looking. Sometimes I go a long way round rather than go through that Number 41 gate at night. It depends on the moon but sometimes you just get that feeling.'

I told him he had just ensured that I'd never feel comfortable opening a gate at night ever again. He laughed. It may have been his plan.

'There's others walking around too. Spirits of my people. But they're all right. You hear them sometimes, outside the door at night making a noise.

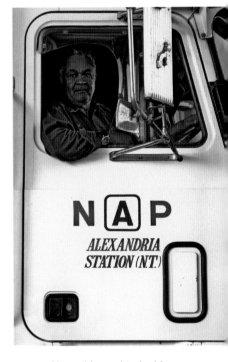

Alexandria road train driver, and Barkly Tableland legend, Johnny Rankine,
(Evan McHugh)

They're just keeping an eye on things.'

J.R. worked his way up from being a stockman. In 1974 he started driving trucks, then spent a year on a grader and a year on a bore truck. Eventually he became the road-train driver. While mechanics were responsible for most of the other vehicles and machines on the station, the road train was his domain. His initials are painted on the side.

'I'm mostly moving cattle around paddocks,' he explained. 'RTA [Road Trains Australia] take cattle away to other stations.'

Driving around the station suited him, he said. He didn't even like going to town any more. However, station life isn't like it once was. He started to talk about the changes, and his smile faded away.

'There used to be an old Aboriginal camp,' he said. 'Not many white fellas. Then they got all these new ideas, got civilised and took them all way.

'My father was a bore mechanic. My mother was cooking in the kitchen. I was one of eight kids. They all started off here but all went away. I'm the only one that stayed at home. My wife and I had five kids. My wife died six years ago. Cancer. Two of the kids are in Katherine; one is a teacher. The other three are in Tennant Creek. They all grew up and went to school. Now they're all working for the government. One of my girls played basketball for Australia and for the Northern Territory.'

I asked him what it was like at the station in years gone by.

'I've known all the managers,' he said. 'Bill Young was the first one: Bill, Long John Olsen, Ross. Bill was a lively old fella, cheeky old fella. He kept an eye on us. We had to stay out of pubs. We had to stay away from the old Aboriginal people. We couldn't go chasing their daughters. They'd watch us. As soon as the sun went down, we'd go to sleep but there were some, they'd still go down. You know how it is.'

We talked about the challenges of driving a road train on the unsealed roads of the station, and he seemed a bit surprised himself that he'd managed to get bogged just the day before.

'All three trailers bogged,' he said. 'I had to unhook and take one load, then come back. It's been eleven or twelve years since I did that. There was some ground that was spongy from the rain a couple of months ago. The trailers were digging in. With a load of heifers, 120–130 tonne is a bit too heavy.'

When he wasn't driving the truck, or doing the maintenance on it, he turned his hand to just about everything, from pulling bores to fighting fires.

'We give the young people a bit of help,' he said. 'We show them how to load cattle onto the truck. The young fellas change tyres, do bearings, drive forklifts but we teach them a little bit when we can. We put them on the right track.'

Aaron Thege mustering 250 head of black Angus with his stockhorse Trapper in the Strzelecki Ranges of Victoria, 2012. Working dogs and horses are still the best way to tackle the steep and ruggedly beautiful country.

(Nicole Emanuel)

When I asked if there was anywhere on the station that particularly appealed to him, he replied, 'This place is pretty good everywhere: there's a bit of scrub gidgee, a bit of desert, timber in places. With three stations it's not really boring.'

J.R. didn't have an answer to what the future held.

'The company has looked after me well,' he said. 'I don't know about retiring. What would I do? I'm happy to keep going while I can.'

Road trainer driver Greg Vinson on Headingly Station, 2011.

(Evan McHugh)

Greg Vinson was the road-train driver on Headingly Station, at the top of Channel Country. When I caught up with him he'd pulled up to give directions to another road-train driver, a contractor from a road transport company, RTA.

They were talking about an accident that had happened the day before, involving a truck on the Plenty Highway. The heavy vehicle laden with cattle had been forced off the unsealed road by a tourist's car and had rolled on its side, killing a number of cattle.

Outback people know that the usual procedure when approaching a road train on a dirt track is to slow right down or stop and give the road train the whole road. If you're smart, you pull over to the windward side of the road so you don't get a dust bath. One of the reasons for stopping is so you avoid having your windshield chipped or broken by a stone thrown up from the road train's many wheels. The other reason is that in many places the ground on the sides of the narrow roads is too soft to support the road train's weight.

Greg wasn't your typical truckie. He'll hate me for saying it but he reminded me of Paddington Bear. He was round-faced and friendly, but he also had a similar hat! He was one of the best blokes I met during my several trips into the outback, which is saying something. He looked to be in his thirties, although due to bouncing in the road train my attempt to take notes recorded his age as something like 8N. The father of three had been a Headingly employee since 2005.

'We came with a five-year plan, which we now have taken out to ten years,' he said. 'We've got a house in Charters Towers that's rented out. This place suits us now.'

Greg was picking up a load of weaners that were yarded up in Moontah Paddock, where a team of contract musterers assisted with loading them. Even the contractors were in a good mood. The five of them were a close-knit team of a husband and wife, two young jillaroos and a jackaroo. They all clearly knew what they were doing. Everyone was too busy to talk much so I helped push cattle up the race. I thought it wiser not to follow them into the drafting pen to coax recalcitrant stock along. I couldn't imagine how anyone would explain to an insurance company how a writer came to be in such a place when a charging beast hit him. I also kept well back from the iron rails of the race, having seen the results of stray hooves flying out to badly bruise or break a leg.

'You sometimes get caught by cattle,' Greg said. 'I got kicked once; it caught me through the rails of the race, fair on the end of the percy. That folded me up all right.'

The weaners were loaded forty to a deck on the six decks of the station's road train, a Mac Titan with a 600-horsepower Caterpillar motor. Once they were loaded, Greg posed for a few pictures, then we were on our way.

Greg was originally from Hughenden, where he did his local schooling before spending two years at Brisbane. He started driving trucks in Townsville on a range of jobs, including carrying station supplies. He used to load wool for a neighbouring property but in 1986 they stopped running sheep because of the cost of labour and falling prices as a result of the wool-stockpile debacle. Most of his driving for Headingly was done on the station.

'I cart about 18 000 head a year to yards then back out to the paddocks,' he said. 'I've also done trips to Longreach, Roma, Toowoomba and South Galway. Last year I did 137 000 kilometres, all on Headingly, except for one trip to Avon Downs and one trip to town [Mount Isa]. I did 220 kilometres one day and never left the station.'

In 2008 he did quite a few trips to save cattle that were in danger of perishing due to the drought that affected the entire region.

'We didn't put stock up the ramp to the top deck because they were too weak,' he said. 'By the end there were only 3000 head left on the property.'

As the landscape slid slowly past, I asked Greg whether he had to keep his speed down to avoid throwing the stock around.

'On dirt we're doing 60 kilometres an hour and even slower,' he said. 'It's about preservation and keeping your gear in good order. The trailers are thirty-one years old. They're pretty tough and hold up well. They were made to last. But tyres get shredded. The stones are small and sharp and pierce tyres. Cheap brands fall apart. You have to get good quality to get the life.'

Slower speeds also mean a saving in fuel, although the cost of running the road train still works out at about $3 per kilometre. Our trip with 240 weaners cost the equivalent of an entire beast, just in moving them from one paddock to another.

With the road train travelling so slowly, even relatively short trips can take considerable time. While there may not be transport inspectors lurking so far from major centres, Greg has done training in fatigue management, and to a degree polices himself.

He also has to contend with some unexpected obstacles. The river crossings can catch out the unwary. Even when it's dry, as it was when we went over the Georgina, negotiating the crossing with a load of skittish weaners and a vehicle with a loaded weight of 120 tonnes calls for considerable skill.

When we were across Greg pulled up to check the stock was all right, then we rolled on past the town of Urandangi, which turned out to be the source of another unexpected hazard.

'One thing you have to watch out for on these roads is stray timber,' Greg said. 'Locals come out to load up with gidgee and sometimes it falls off on the way back to town. You can be driving through open country and come across a log in the middle of the road.'

When we started talking about his time at Headingly, something of a recurring theme emerged.

'Steve has been good to me,' Greg said. 'AA has been good to us. Because we've got kids we go to Mount Isa quite a lot. There are no other families here, no interaction, so we try to get them out a lot. The kids go to school but we like to keep them occupied and seeing different things all the time. But it's not isolated here. There are plenty of interesting things and you can talk to people. In the cities you don't know your neighbours.'

Back at the station yard, the stock camp was processing the weaners. Sam the pilot was operating the cradle, Joe and Anna were doing ear tags, John was dehorning, Lucy was castrating, Troy was the leg man, Dominic was branding, and Harriet (who was visiting her sister Lucy but got roped into doing some stock work) was sending them up the race and vaccinating. For the weaners, it was a stressful experience but the stock camp was well drilled and each weaner was processed in as little as 30 seconds. The faster it could be done, the better it was for all concerned. The only delay was when I tried for a shot of the brand going on and they paused for a few seconds to help me.

While they were doing that, Pat the head stockman was keeping an eye on things nearby, while shoeing horses.

When everyone was about to knock off for the day, a road train pulled in with another load of weaners. Nobody left until they were all safely unloaded.

While I had a yarn with station manager Steve Hagan, two jillaroos drove up in a truck loaded with horses. They turned towards the loading ramp so quickly you could hear the horses slipping in the back over the sound of grinding gears. They then started manoeuvring to get close to the ramp.

'This is about to go to shit,' Steve said as he looked on. 'You can tell by the smiles.'

However, before the situation turned unpleasant, Steve went over and supervised the unloading. He showed the young women what to do, made sure the horses were unloaded unharmed, and betrayed no annoyance that he should have to get involved.

While he did that, I looked around at the rest of the staff, going about the last jobs of another long day – brushing horses, feeding stock in the yards, putting away equipment That's when it struck me. It was late, they were tired, but they were still in a good mood. Everyone around me was actually happy. It may have been a subtle thing, but they were enjoying what they were doing. Then they headed off for a beer and a shower, while Steve banged about closing gates and checking water troughs.

Much has changed at Victoria River Downs over the years. Once over 40 000 square kilometres in size, it has since been divided into several smaller, more manageable properties. The station called Victoria River Downs is now just over 2000 square kilometres.

'Managing a property like this is about being more efficient,' manager Rusty Richter said. 'Ten or fifteen years ago, the stock camp numbered twelve to fourteen. Now it's seven. We use machinery to be more efficient, helicopters on a large scale. The costs are high but helicopter hours are the lowest cost, compared to diesel and wages that are the highest.'

I asked him whether he struggles to get people to work in such a remote location.

'It's not hard getting staff, it's hard getting *good* staff,' he said. 'It's not like [TV show] *McLeod's Daughters*. That's been good because it gets people to leave the city, but we've had girls come out here and they're shocked by the reality.'

When considering applicants Rusty checks their references but also looks to see if they've played any team sports. Working in a stock camp means being part of a team. In fact, I'd already heard staff referred to as crew, and seen them behave with the same coordinated purpose I'd experienced while racing yachts.

Rusty also finds it hard to keep a good stock camp together when the station closes down for the wet. Some people are prepared to wait for work to start up in the next season, but others find alternative employment and don't want to leave it. He also regards the cattle industry as one where older and long-term staff are becoming increasingly rare.

'Young people now are looking to move up,' he said. 'They want to take the next opportunity. We've got one staff member who has been with Heytesbury [the company that owns VRD] eight years. Our oldest employee is our grader driver; he's fifty. But look at me. I'm thirty-two and I know I don't want to be knocked around by cranky cattle when I'm fifty.'

An early morning start on Lake Nash, Barkly Tableland, Northern Territory, 2008. While some may disparage Generation Y for a lack of get up and go, when they are working on stock camps you have to be up before dawn to see where they've got up and gone.

(Scott Bridle)

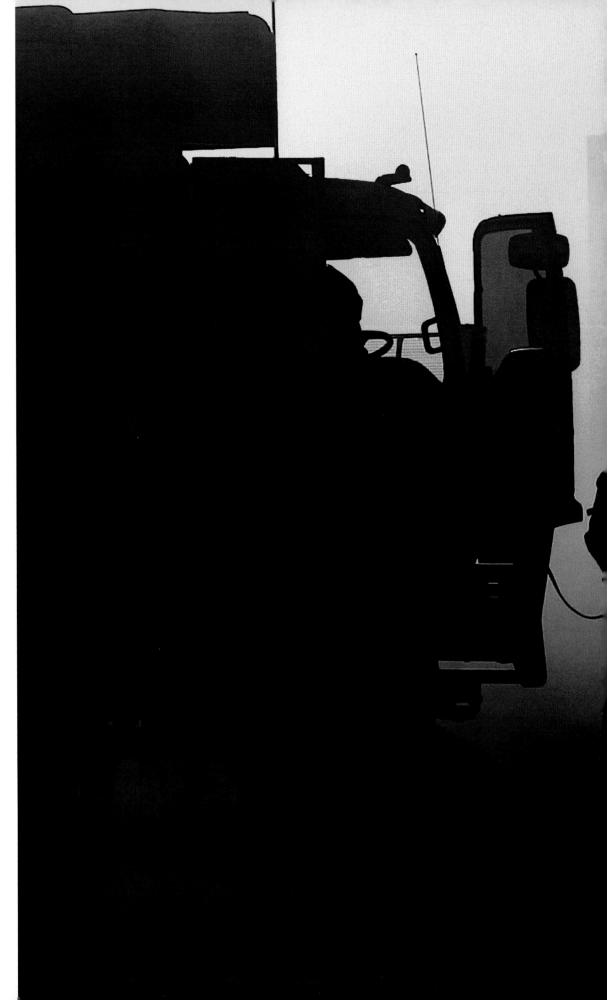

On the ground, the station uses a mixture of motorbikes and horses. Helmets are compulsory.

'It's company policy,' Rusty said, 'a sackable offence. Everyone also has to say where there are going and when they'll be back. They've all got shoulder patches with UHF radios. Even if I go somewhere, I tell Julie what I'm up to, in case something goes wrong.'

Heytesbury is an equal-opportunity employer but Rusty reckoned that there are still gender dynamics that have to be managed.

'When you've got two women in a stock camp, they'll team up,' he said, 'but when you've got three, two team up and leave the third isolated. However, if it's all blokes, it can get a bit feral, especially in stock camps.'

Staff usually work six days a week, then have a day off, which Rusty usually tries to give them, no matter how flat-out the station might be. Ultimately, they have to have a day off after thirteen on.

'You can't really work regular hours,' he said. 'Some days you can work eight hours but others it's fifteen. If you've got cattle in yards, you've got to get them out. If you work regular hours, you get behind.'

Headingly Station head stockman Pat Barrett shaping horseshoes in the homestead yards, 2011.
(Evan McHugh)

On nearby Wave Hill, scene of the famous Wave Hill walk-off, it was a similar story. The station is a highly efficient modern operation, with management practices to match. While visiting the property in 2011 I asked manager Greg Dakin if the station was an 'equal opportunity employer'.

'We employ women,' he replied, cutting to the chase. 'I actually worked on a station where I was the only male. It had a head stockwoman and all-female crew. It wasn't planned that way but that's how it worked out. My approach is I pay women the same pay as the men but they're treated the same. They can't say I can't lift that or I can't do that. If they don't like it, they go.'

He also accepted that most young people won't stay long. They want to see the world and don't want to be working for the same boss for five or six years. That said, he explained, 'We like to get young people because we can form them. They're better than a lot of kids who've been raised on places like this, because there are a lot of things they won't do. They think it's beneath them.'

Greg drove me out to one of the station's yards and I soon found that he meant what he said about women having to do the same as the men. Over at the calf cradle, they were branding, castrating, dehorning and earmarking calves. When one particularly athletic calf managed to turn himself backwards in the cradle, they were called upon to employ considerable strength to turn him back around. However, I noticed that when something like that happened, other members of the stock camp moved in to help, without having to be asked.

Driving back from the yards, when I climbed back into the ute after opening and closing yet another gate, I mentioned that figuring out how some of them worked was a bit of an intelligence test.

'Some of those old gates have killed stockmen in days gone by,' Greg said. 'They've got their fingers caught and didn't have the strength with one arm to lift the bar. They haven't had a knife to cut their fingers off, so they stayed there till they died.'

These days, such a thing is virtually impossible. As with all the stations I visited, the whereabouts of all staff are constantly monitored. If someone doesn't call, the search begins.

We weren't far from the station when we came upon a mob of weaners being poked along the road, just to get them used to being around people. I got out to take some photos and risked lying in front of them while the stock walked quietly past and around me. The young Brahmans didn't seem at all concerned, although I sensed Greg was having kittens behind me. Greg pointed out a young boy of about twelve droving the cattle along with two jillaroos. It was his son, Billy.

As the sun set and the cattle slowly walked along, the young fella looked to be in his element. He was supposed to be doing his schoolwork but instead was getting life experience you'd never find in books. As the stock drifted away from us, it was hard not to feel he had already gained something someone like me would always lack.

It's one thing to talk about stockmen mustering using modern methods. It's quite another to see it actually being done. Near central Australia's New Crown Station, I got the opportunity to do so first hand. The adjustment paddock being mustered was north of the town of Finke.

The manager's wife, Colleen Costello, showed me how to get there. We found the deserted stock camp and continued on in search of manager Don and his mustering crew. We managed to pick up a helicopter on the radio and moments later the pilot, Danny Rickard, landed beside us for a quick yarn before giving us directions. He then flew off while we continued on our way. For Colleen, it was a routine procedure, but when we got going again I pointed out that to an outsider it was one of those pinch-yourself experiences.

As we went bush in search of the musterers, I gingerly picked the LandCruiser's way around mulga stakes that could puncture my tyres in a moment and negotiated vertical drops where Cyclone Yasi's floodwaters had cut deep channels that could destroy the suspension. Eventually Colleen heard the cattle and the motorbikes in the distance and we pulled up to wait for them to come to us.

Another helicopter landed and pilot Rodney Mengel came over to say hello. Rodney was the burly, grey-bearded and jovial owner of Mengel's Heliservices and was there to assist with the mustering. He was also training a new pilot hoping to join his company. The new guy was flying around some distance away, looking for strays. With a chuckle Rodney said, 'He shouldn't get into any trouble. There's no cattle over there.'

Rodney said he had no problems getting pilots but was often disappointed by their work ethic, or lack of it. By way of example, he told of one fellow he'd agreed to give a try who then asked about pay and relocation expenses.

'I'm offering my helicopter and all the running costs while he gets experience, and that's not enough,' Rodney sighed. 'This fella I've got now is a bit different. He turned up one day after I made him the offer. He's keen and if he's any good, he'll go far.'

The mob was getting quite close and Rodney headed back to his chopper and took off.

Shortly after, the first lines of cattle came stringing through the scrub. Quite a few of the beasts were unbranded and they were big, meaning they had not set eyes on people for some years, if ever. The only predictable thing about them was their eagerness to escape. Don Costello pulled up in an incredibly battered ute and swapped places with Colleen. The idea was for me to have a chat while we drove along.

Don's focus on the job at hand was intense. His mustering crew was a mixture of experienced hands and young stockmen who'd been backpacking around Australia only a few months before. Don was constantly on the radio, especially to his inexperienced staff, coaching them on what to do.

The herd was volatility incarnate. One moment they were walking along quietly, the next a breakaway charged into the scrub pursued by utes and motorcycles. It wasn't hard to understand how broken collarbones and impalement on protruding branches were common injuries among stockmen. At times, they needed to focus on several things at once – cattle, trees and creek washouts – while moving at speed.

In breaks between high-speed manoeuvres, Don managed to talk, with somewhat divided attention.

'We get staff from all over, including backpackers,' he said, 'but I prefer tradesmen. They have a better work ethic and it's less about adventure. They can also do things when they're not doing cattle work, which can be a real bonus. A company called Outback Packer trains backpackers for station work but the boys don't like it when they've just got someone trained up and then they go.'

I asked if he used fixed-wing aircraft to muster.

'We only use choppers,' he said. 'I have a pilot's licence, to make it easier to get around, but I don't muster. I prefer to leave it to the specialists.'

I noted that most of the motorbike riders were wearing hats, rather than helmets.

'We provide helmets for motorcycle riders but don't insist they use them,' he said, admitting that he might soon have to. 'The main problem is they get hot and you can't hear the radio. The radio is on the shoulder pad, not in the helmet.'

There was no question about having to hear the radio. During mustering there is usually quite a lot of radio chatter (not always constructive), although for this crew it was very calm and specific. Each vehicle or rider had a position that was based on where they were in relation to the mob, with twelve o'clock being the direction the mob was heading, three o'clock the right flank, six o'clock the rear, and nine o'clock the left flank. So an instruction like 'watch those two at four' meant the crew near the right rear of the mob had to watch for a potential breakaway.

From time to time Don called a halt to give the mob a bit of a rest. To my mind it gave them a chance to regroup for the next escape attempt.

'The worst accident we've had was my son-in-law, Ben, who had a double break at the top and bottom of his leg when he came off a motorbike,' Don said. 'He was out of action for six months.'

The sun was getting low when we finally reached the yards where the cattle were to be held for the night. There the mob mustered by the ground crew was joined by another mob mustered by the choppers. Double the herd meant double the fun and there were breakaways in all directions, with vehicles and choppers charging everywhere in pursuit or to cut them off. Even when the animals settled down, it was a tricky business pushing cattle that had never seen stockyards through the gates. Once it was done, 200 head crowded into the furthest corner of the yard, as far as they could get from the people who had been pursuing them all day.

The tension of mustering ebbed away as dust rose from the yards, lit by the setting sun and framed by the backdrop of a dramatic table-topped hill ringed by cliffs of red stone. Across the plain the grass called neverfail was changing from pale yellow to gold. Central Australia could be a harsh and unforgiving place but just then it was beautiful.

Back at the stock camp, Colleen offered to take me back to the comforts of the New Crown homestead, but I was interested in spending the night in the stock camp. She gave me a funny look, like until that moment I'd seemed pretty sensible, and left me to my fate.

It was just on dusk as everyone rolled into camp in their various utes.

Danny Rickard was already there having flown back in his chopper. The bikes were left back at the yards, ready for the morning. No one needed to be told what to do as firewood was collected, the campfire was kindled, and vehicles manoeuvred so their trays could be used as tables and the spotlights on their rollbars could illuminate the camp.

The rump of a beast that until recently had been fattening on central Australian pasture was cut into steaks, which were soon sizzling on a hot plate. Wood was piled up for the night and the next morning. A bucket of water was put out so people could wash before dinner. A few beers were passed around and a billy was put on the fire to boil water for tea. Most of the stock crew carried their swags over to the fire and used them for seats while they ate dinner – steak and bread.

We'll light our camp-fires where we may, and yarn beside their blaze;
The jingling hobble-chains shall make a music through the days.
And while the tucker-bags are right, and we've a stick of weed,
A swagman shall be welcome to a pipe-full and a feed.

Harry 'Breaker' Morant, 'West By North Again'

After their meal they had a few cups of tea and tuned in a radio to listen to a game of football. They talked about cattle for a little while and then, at around eight o'clock, they started getting ready to turn in. The radio was turned off, even though the game was far from over. I was expecting them to roll their swags out around the fire but instead everyone drove their utes away or walked off in separate directions to find a quiet spot to sleep on their own. Some rolled out their swags on the trays of their utes so the rodents that were everywhere due to a mouse plague wouldn't bother them.

By 8:15 p.m. all was quiet, but for the distant snoring of sleeping stockmen and the constant sound of scurrying rodents. Far above, the night sky was full of stars. Down below, the mice were close to matching them in number.

Sleep came easily, although in the early morning I was woken by a bull that came groaning and bellowing around the camp. After half an hour, it took its mournful noise beyond earshot, only for it to be replaced by the blood-curdling screams of a fox.

The eastern horizon was just turning from black to deep blue when the stock camp started to wake. There was no rousing call. By 5:30 a.m. everyone was up and about, emerging from their swags fully clothed. It turned out that two fellas in the stock camp didn't have swags: one had slept in a ute, or had

tried to, while the other slept in his clothes on the ground.

Breakfast comprised sausages, bread and tea. Its preparation and consumption was a matter of a few minutes, by which time there was just enough light to see clearly. Having slept as long as possible, they'd timed their waking to perfection. The camp was away and over at the yards by dawn.

Stockmen dehorning cattle in yards at Montejinni Station, Northern Territory, 1955. Such procedures may cause stress to an animal but the benefit is that it prevents subsequent injuries to stock and stockmen.
(Howard Truran Collection, NT Library, PH0406/0234)

AN
AUSTRALIAN
ICON

When the Olympic Games came to Sydney in the year 2000, there was a lot riding on the first few seconds of the Opening Ceremony. The eyes of the world would be watching, and that crucial first impression that would identify these Olympics as distinctly Australian would set the tone for everything to follow. What could possibly convey a uniquely Australian image that would be instantly recognisable in all of the countries of the world, where an audience of billions was tuning in? It was one of the toughest calls in show business, and there were no second chances. It had to be big. It had to grab the world's attention. It had to be perfect.

Unfortunately, just one month before that pivotal moment, amid final preparations for an event that was costing millions of dollars and drawing thousands of athletes and spectators from around the globe, the Olympic Opening Ceremony organisers had come up empty-handed. Yet the show had to go on. So, on 15 September 2000, Sydney Olympic Stadium darkened as giant screens around the packed arena started the final countdown ...

For more than two years prior to the Opening Ceremony, the organisers had been assembling a cast of thousands, supported by hundreds of technicians, to stage half a dozen distinct segments that conveyed the heritage and identity of the host nation.

One segment was a tribute to the horses and riders, stockmen and women, whose courage, resourcefulness and endurance have been amply demonstrated in the preceding chapters of this book. Helping bring that segment together was a down-to-earth horse trainer named Steve Jefferys.

Born in 1956, Steve was from the semi-rural Sydney district around Terrey Hills, where he'd developed an interest in horses from the age of twelve. He was soon visiting the nearby 'ranch' run by singer and bushman Smokey Dawson, learning to ride on weekends and doing odd jobs. When he left school, he worked for a short time for the horseman John Pinnell, who taught him to break in horses. Then he went to work at Randwick, under John Drennan, breaking horses for racehorse trainer Tommy Smith. Eventually, his horsemanship took him around the world, delivering racehorses. It was a great life, and one that required plenty of skill, especially in loading nervous thoroughbreds onto cargo planes.

Steve worked in the U.S. for three years before returning to Australia in the early 1980s, still only in his early twenties. He eventually married and got a job in, of all things, dry cleaning. However, it was the end of his marriage, in 1994, when he was thirty-eight, that left him questioning his future and set him on course for the greatest test of his life.

'Almost instantly I felt like going back to horses,' he recalls.

He rang one of the girls he'd known at Smokey Dawson's ranch, Sandy Langsford, who'd gone on to become one of the first women in the New South Wales Mounted Police, breaking in horses and training them for police work, and teaching other constables how to ride.

'I'm interested in getting back into the horse business,' he told her.

She said, 'I've got this horse I want broken in.'

Soon he and Sandy had set up in the horse business together, teaching and attending competitions in dressage and stockhorse events, especially with a smart young stallion named Jamieson. It was at an event in Grafton that Steve bumped into another old friend from his Smokey Dawson days, horse master Tony Jablonski.

Tony said, 'I'd like you to help me do this project.'

'That was two years out from the Olympics,' Steve recalls. 'And it was all confidential in those days, it was almost just an idea, it wasn't even really going to happen. He wanted me to help him find the horses, horsemen. I was the Sydney person and he was in Queensland so I did all the work with SOCOG [Sydney Organising Committee for the Olympic Games] at the stadium.'

While maintaining secrecy about exactly what they were doing, they started advertising for riders who wanted to be in 'Olympic celebrations'. When people turned up for trials, they were asked to sign a confidentiality agreement. Then they were told that the celebration was actually a segment in the Opening Ceremony, based on that iconic text of the bush, 'The Man From Snowy River'.

The initial plan devised by artistic director David Atkins and segment designer Ignatius Jones called for 200 horses and riders. However, when the horsemen measured the space available, they realised 200 horses was far too many. Gradually the number was reduced until it settled on 120 horses and riders who would perform a number of choreographed moves en masse.

Meanwhile, the night of the Opening Ceremony was fast approaching.

Two months before the Ceremony, two 'boot camps' were held for the riders, at Scone, north-west of Sydney. It was at these three-day weekend sessions that the finishing touches were put to the segment. It was also at the second boot camp, in July 2000, that the stakes were raised considerably.

As Steve recalls: 'There'd been talk of different things at the very opening. At the July boot camp the guys from SOCOG were there. They said, "You guys are going to open the Olympic Games."'

The organisers realised that the horsemen were perfect for the image of Australia they wanted to convey. The Australian bush hero, the stockman, was a figure all Australians could identify with, and the rest of the world recognised it as well. Yet they still needed that initial impact.

Steve Jefferys, the horseman chosen to embody the Man from Snowy River in the opening ceremony of the Sydney 2000 Olympic Games.

(Nicole Emanuel)

Says Steve: 'They had ideas of several horses coming in fast, and they canned all those. They wanted something out there that was going to take everyone's attention while all these horses suddenly appeared. They decided they were gonna have a rearing horse.'

The organisers even had the horse that was going to do it. Tony Jablonski had a horse and rider up in Queensland that he'd used in various movies. The notion, however, interested Steve. 'I thought at the time, "Gee, I wouldn't mind riding that horse. That'd be all right."'

It was when the Opening Ceremony organisers flew to Queensland to check on their rearing horse that they found it was nothing like what they wanted. Worse still, they were now left with a gaping hole at the head of their program. So, a month before the Opening Ceremony was due to take place, Ignatius Jones rang Steve.

'Have you got a horse that can do this job?' he asked.

The organisers assumed that Steve would put forward his magnificent stallion, Jamieson. He was the kind of animal they had in mind, 'black and wild looking'. He'd also been taught to rear on command, but not with Steve in the saddle. However, Jamieson was already committed. He was in quarantine because he was going to be part of the entertainment at the Olympic Equestrian Centre, mixing with horses from all over the world.

Steve was honest with Jones. 'It's too risky,' he told the man who, at the time, had no opening for the greatest show on Earth. 'The risk of getting a horse to rear up under that sort of pressure at that instant is pie in the sky.'

He had a point. However, Steve soon heard that Jones was asking around, trying to find anyone who had a horse that could rear. With three weeks to go, things had reached the stage where what was needed was someone who could show some of that legendary stockman spirit and resourcefulness, someone who was prepared to step forward in a tight situation. Or as Steve put it, 'Well, if they're going to do it, I may as well do it.'

He rang Jones and said, 'We've got a horse here that has never reared, but I think he probably could. Give me a week and I'll let you know how he's going.'

Then he and Sandy went down to the arena where they had another horse, named Ammo.

'An obnoxious character,' is how Steve describes him. 'He's what you call a rig, which means he's never been castrated properly. So he thinks he's a stallion even though he's classified as a gelding.

'He didn't care about anyone. He was easily distracted; you'd go out somewhere and he'd look over here and look over there. But because he was strong and didn't like being bossed, I thought, "Well, let's see what happens."'

'So we went down here and I said to Sandy, "You just tap him on the feet." That's one way to put them under pressure, which is maintained until they give you the correct answer, and you reward them when they do. He went up a little bit and we shoved a carrot in his mouth. And he thought, "Oh, this is all right." So he said, "If that gets me a carrot, try this!" And he almost instantly started rearing.'

The two horse trainers were delighted, but Steve was still cautious. It was one thing to get a horse to rear in his own arena, quite another to get it to happen in an Olympic Stadium before 100 000 people. So it wasn't until two days later that he rang Ignatius Jones and said, 'Things are going okay. This horse might make it.'

Three days later, he rang again and said, 'Iggy, you can come and have a look at him. He's going all right.'

Steve recalls the visit of the worried folk from SOCOG: 'I set out a video and we ran him at the video camera and reared him up, and they were ecstatic. They were saying, "This is fantastic! He's the horse!"'

After they'd left, Steve confided in Sandy. 'That's a lot of crap. They've got other horses that they've got in mind for this.'

Meanwhile, he continued working with Ammo. Steve the perfectionist knew the horse had a long way to go: 'He would come in and rear four times out of five, and that wasn't good enough. If number five came up on the day, I'd be in big trouble.'

He also needed the rear to be spectacular, wild and big. That was part of the reason the original horse had been excluded. So the schooling continued. And then, all too soon, there were only ten days before the Opening Ceremony.

Another boot camp. Was there another horse or were Steve and Ammo going to open the Olympics? Of more concern for Steve, Ammo was tiring. He wasn't used to all the work and his rears were becoming intermittent. Steve was so concerned he turned to one of the other riders at boot camp, John Pinnell, the man who'd taught him to break in horses more than twenty years before. The Olympics were such a big thing for Pinnell that he'd come out of retirement just to ride.

'I've got a problem,' Steve told him. 'This horse is starting to back off a bit.'

Pinnell worked with Steve to get the horse rearing again, but he also worked on giving Steve confidence. He kept telling him it was going to be okay.

'And the big thing was there was no other horse there,' Steve recalls. 'There was no backup.'

By then, though, they were going into the stadium every night for rehearsals.

'I'd go in each night and he was going pretty good,' Steve recalls. 'He did some good stuff and one night he got up, and he stood there, and it felt like an eternity. And the SOCOG people go, "That's it! That's what we want!"'

Steve still wasn't confident that he was going to launch the Opening Ceremony, even as they rehearsed doing that very thing. He was convinced that, if it wasn't working, his entry would be dropped at the last minute. They couldn't have a horse ride out before an audience of billions and look stupid.

'I wasn't convinced until the first dress rehearsal,' he recalls. 'The first dress rehearsal we went out and I said to Sandy, "We're going to do this. We're going to open the Olympic Games."'

Throughout those tense days, Steve lost a lot of weight. While in boot camp with several hundred people, all of them living on top of each other, he'd also caught the flu. It got to the stage where most of the riders were sick, exhausted by the 9 a.m. starts and 3 a.m. finishes.

Not surprisingly, Steve started losing sleep.

'I'd wake up at night and I'd have nightmares. One was the horse standing on the whip. Simply that he wouldn't go up. Things like not stopping square. How to hold the whip. How would I hold the reins so there was no chance of not stopping him? And then my hat blowing off. Originally I was just going to rear the horse up. Then they said you're going to crack the whip and I just thought they'll have a mechanical sound and they'll cue it. "No, you can't do

that because it won't look right. You've got to do it." So they miked up the
horse. All these blokes, all cow cockies, they all came around giving me their
whips to try. I'm standing up on this 44-gallon drum, trying all these whips
because I wanted to get the whip that would sound the best. So we came
down with this whip, a young boy's whip it was.'

Finally, the moment arrived. Weak from the flu, sleep deprived and
considerably thinner than he'd been ten days earlier, Steve mounted Ammo
and prepared to open the 2000 Olympic Games.

'I was sick on the night but it's funny how adrenalin gives you the power
to do something that you think you can't do. By then I was concerned about
stopping Ammo. He was getting so powerful it was going to take a lot of
strength to control him.

'I must have started to transmit some sort of excitement. He was agitated.
He knew, because he'd done it so many times, he was going out and he
was getting excited and started to run backwards in the entrance. And I'm
thinking, "The countdown's going to start and there's horses piled up behind
me waiting to come out." And I'm trying to settle him down and get him
under control because I'm waiting for this girl to give me the signal. It was a
lot happening in a short space of time.'

Then came the sign.

'I blanked out from looking at anything. It was an image of noise and
flashes and all I was focusing on was what I had to do. There could have
been a kangaroo sat beside me; I wouldn't have seen it. I was that focused on
doing the job. He was unbelievably strong. He was just so on fire, which was
the look they wanted, they wanted this wild image coming out. He came out
at a million miles an hour, jumped up because there was a lip up onto the
arena. He flew up and I'm thinking, "This thing's not going to stop", and I'm
really working overtime at making it get to the middle. It was an immense
amount of energy going into making this few seconds happen. I'm talking
to myself as I went out, stop, drop the whip, crack the whip, and I was really
oblivious to anything.

'And he knew once he'd stopped that the next thing was to rear; he'd done
it so many times. He had so much energy coming out that the chances of
him not rearing at that stage weren't real high. He was pretty pumped up,
like I was. And he ran in, I cued him for the rear. He went up once. Then he
went up again, and the second one was a good one.'

As the television images and thousands of photos taken at that moment
still show, the rear was huge. The massive black animal was power incarnate,
an expression of the ultimate in horsemanship. And on his back, the man
from Snowy River had come alive, to welcome the world to Sydney. The

THE AUSTRALIAN STOCKHORSE

As few as six horses (some accounts suggest eight) arrived with the First Fleet in 1788, and the preference was for draught horses rather than riding horses. However, it wasn't long before horses started arriving in Australia in significant numbers; there were 300 in the colony in 1802. It quickly became clear that the Australian climate and grasses were extremely well suited to the horses' development. In particular, their endurance compared favourably to that of horses in Europe. This particular quality was invaluable to stockmen facing the challenges of a country the size of Australia. Horses were eventually working in nearly every environment: Tasmania, along the Great Dividing Range from the Australian Alps to tropical far north Queensland, the vast stations of central, northern and western Australia, and everywhere in between.

The Australian stockhorse emerged as an intelligent, hard-working animal with plenty of strength and stamina. While breeds such as the Waler (a New South Wales stockhorse) can be clearly identified, mixtures of breeds also fit the description of an Australian stockhorse. The man from Snowy River's 'small and weedy beast a little like a racehorse undersized, with a touch of Timor Pony, three-parts thoroughbred at least' is perhaps the best-known example.

At times the quality of Australian horses has suffered from poor or non-existent breeding practices. However, recent years have seen a renewed interest in the Australian stockhorse and emphasis on preserving and improving on its best qualities. In 1971 the Australian Stockhorse Society was formed to preserve and promote the bloodlines of the Australian stockhorse. The Society now has 9500 members and 180 000 registered horses.

Aboriginal stockman and stockhorse, Brunette Downs Station, 1966. While their characteristics may differ, the prime quality of all Australian stockhorses is endurance in even the toughest conditions.
(National Archives of Australia, A1200, L55932)

stadium was filled with camera flashes, the world's attention was gripped by the Olympics from that moment, and it was held until the Closing Ceremony sixteen days later.

The organisers had done it – they'd found the image that identified Australia to the world. They'd brought Australia's bush legend to life. While attention was focused on Steve and Ammo, the stadium filled with 120 other riders, and the Olympics had begun.

Back in the tunnel, Steve somehow managed to get the mighty Ammo to stop without trampling the other performers waiting to go out for their segments. 'The minute I was inside that tunnel I thought, "I've done it." I remember the music playing as the other horses were coming in, the sense of pride at that time and the emotion of what these guys were doing. I can feel it now; it was incredible.

'The honour wasn't something I was thinking about at that time. It was a great relief. We all realised what we'd done afterwards. We went back and you could see the crowds of people and the excitement that the whole Olympics Opening had lit and that we'd started. A lot of elderly people that saw it were extremely emotional. People who were overseas at the time told me later how it made them proud to be Australian.'

Australia has come a long way since the first days of European settlement. Today, it's one of the most urbanised populations on Earth, and the reality of existence for most Australians is far removed from the bush. Yet many of us still identify with the world beyond the urban fringe. Walk into a fashionable shopping mall, and among the Italian suits and French couture, you'll find bush outfitters R.M. Williams, the clothing chain established by Sidney Kidman's saddler. Hundreds of thousands of people from cities and the country ride in competitions designed to keep the traditions and skills of stockmen alive. And of course, young Australians are still heading out to work for a year or two and find out what it means to be a real stockman.

When Steve rode out to open the Sydney Olympics in September 2000, it was anything but a solo effort. He carried with him the memories and heritage of a nation that reveres the image of the stockman. Anyone who could identify with and be proud of the skills, courage and resourcefulness of the Australian stockman was in the saddle that night. And Ammo was strong enough to carry us all.

The man from Snowy River is now part of Australia's cultural identity. We may travel far from the outback and bush, we may never learn to ride, and we may never know the freedom of a stockman's life. Yet it's always there. It's that secret part of us that tells us who we really are.

SOURCES

TEXT SOURCES

All About Australians, Yewen Publishing, Sydney, 4 January 1904.

Anon., Jack Riley, *Corryong Courier*, July 23 1914; 20 January 1949, and undated issues.

Anon., 'Death Of A Stockman', *South Australian Register*, 20 January 1893.

Anon.,'Death Of Jack Riley', *The Argus*, July 17, 1914.

Anon., 'The Languid North', *Townsville Daily Bulletin*, 2 November 1926.

Anon., Sackville Kidman obituary, *The Critic*, 8 July 1899.

Anon., Sidney Kidman, *Adelaide Observer*, 5 September 1903.

Anon., Sidney Kidman, *The Argus*, 2, 3 and 5 September 1935.

Anon., 'Pastoral Occupation of Northern Territory', *Northern Territory Times and Gazette*, Saturday 4 June 1881, page 3.

Anon., 'Tyson', *The Bulletin*, 17 December 1898.

Anon., 'The Tyson Interview', *The Brisbane Courier*, 8 December 1893.

Anon , 'With the Cattle King', *The Adelaide Observer*, 28 July 1928.

Barker, Hector, *Droving Days*, Hesperian, Carlisle, 1994.

Bowen, J., Kidman, *The Forgotten King*, Angus and Robertson, Pymble, 1987. Extracts by permission Jill Bowen.

Brodribb, William, *Recollections of an Australian Squatter*, John Woods and Co, Sydney, 1883.

Buchanan, Bobbie, *In the Tracks of Old Bluey*, Central Queensland University Press, Rockhampton, 1997.

Buchanan, Gordon, *Packhorse and Waterhole*, Angus and Robertson, Sydney, 1933.

Buchanan, Gordon, 'Pioneers of the Far North', *Stock and Station Journal*, various issues January–February 1922.

Bull, John Wrathall, *Early Experiences Of Life In South Australia*, E. S. Wigg and Son, Adelaide, 1884, facsimile edition Libraries Board of South Australia (source of Bonney's account).

Canning, Alfred, Report to WA Mines Department, 10 January 1907.

Carmody, Jean, *Early Days of the Upper Murray*, Shoestring Press, Wangaratta, 1981.

Carter, Jeff, *In The Tracks Of The Cattle*, Angus and Robertson, Sydney, 1968.

Caust, Peter, 'The Multi-Colour Kids Of Anna Creek', *Australian Women's Weekly*, 28 April 1976.

Costello, Michael, *The Life of John Costello*, Dymocks Book Arcade, Sydney, 1930.

Cunningham, Chris, *The Blue Mountains Rediscovered*, Kangaroo Press, Kenthurst, 1996.

Denholm, Zita, *T.Y.S.O.N.: The Life and Times of James Tyson, Pastoral Pioneer*, Triple D Books, Wagga Wagga, 2002.

Dwyer, Barb., 'The Largest Cattle Station In The World', *Sydney Morning Herald*, 7 June 1947.

Farwell, George, *Land of Mirage*, Cassell, Sydney, 1950.

Gard, Ronele and Eric, *Canning Stock Route: A Traveller's Guide* (3rd edition), Western Desert Guides, Wembley Downs, 2009.

Giles, Alfred, *Exploring in the Seventies*, W. K. Thomas, Adelaide, 1926.

Heyer, John, *The Back of Beyond*, Shell Film Unit, 1954 (available on DVD through the RFDS).

Hill, Ernestine, *The Territory*, Angus and Robertson, Sydney, 1951.

Historical Research Pty Ltd, *Heritage of the Birdsville and Strzelecki Tracks*, South Australian Department of Environment and Heritage, Adelaide, 2002.

Hueneke, Klaus, *People of the Australian High Country*, Tabletop Press, Palmerston ACT, 1997.

Idriess, Ion, *The Cattle King*, Angus and Robertson, Sydney, 1936.

Idriess, Ion, *Flynn of the Inland*, Angus and Robertson, Sydney, 1932.

Kain, Kevin, *The First Overlanders*, Gould Books, Ridgehaven SA, 1991, (includes transcripts of Joseph Hawdon and Charles Bonney's accounts).

Lewis, Darrell, *The Murranji Track, Ghost Road of the Drovers*, Central Queensland University Press, Rockhampton, 2007.

Lhotsky, John, *A Journey from Sydney to the Australian Alps*, J. Innes, Sydney, 1835.

Litchfield, Lois, *Marree and the Tracks Beyond*, L. Litchfield, Marree, 1983.

Loyau, George E., *Notable South Australians*, G. E. Loyau, Adelaide, 1885.

Lunney, Bob, *1500 Down The Murranji*, Crawford House, Adelaide, 1998.

Madigan, Cecil, *Crossing the Dead Heart*, Georgian House, Melbourne, 1946.

Mahood, Marie, *Legends of the Outback*, Central Queensland University Press, Rockhampton, 2002.

Merritt, John, *Losing Ground: Grazing in the Snowy Mountains, 1944–1969*, Turalla Press, Canberra, 2007.

Mintern, Tex, 'A Cattle-man Gives a First-hand Account of One of Australia's Most Arduous Jobs', *The Argus Week-End Magazine*, 15 November 1939.

Mitchell, T.W., *Corryong And The Man From Snowy River District*, Wilkinson Printers for R. Boyes, Albury, 1981.

Mollison, Alexander Fullerton, *An Overlanding Diary*, Mast Gully Press, Melbourne, 1980.

Paterson, Andrew 'Banjo', 'T.Y.S.O.N.', *Australasian Pastoralists' Review*, 18 December 1898.

Peck, Harry, *Memoirs of a Stockman*, Stockland Press, Melbourne, 1942.

Philips, Amy, 'Droving Backwards', *ABC Rural*, broadcast 10 June 2009.

Smith, Eleanor, *The Beckoning West: The Story of H. S. Trotman and the Canning Stock Route*, St George Books, Perth, 1966.

Tolcher, Helen, *Conrick of Nappa Merrie*, Helen Tolcher, Linden Park, 1997.

Troughton, Elwyn, *Red Jack*, self-published, Mareeba, 1995.

Wells, L., *Journal of the Calvert Scientific Exploring Expedition, 1896–7*, Government Printer, Perth, 1902 (facsimile edition published by Hesperian Press, 1993).

Williams, R. M., *Beneath Whose Hand*, Macmillan, Melbourne, 1984.

Williams, R. M., *I Once Met a Man*, Angus and Robertson, Sydney, 1989.

Overleaf: Bob Morrison, a head stockman for Dotswood station, snuggled down in his sleeping bag for a few hours rest, his night horse and saddle ready for any emergency should the cattle rush, 1961.

(W. Brindle, National Archives of Australia, A1200, L39278)

LIVESTOCK MILESTONES

1788   Arrival of First Fleet with small herds and flocks of cattle, sheep, goats and poultry.

1797   First merino sheep introduced to Australia.

1840   Blue heeler cattle dog developed at Muswellbrook, NSW.

1858   First Peppin merino flock (large framed, heavily wooled, drought-resistant breed) established at Deniliquin.

1858   Pleuropneumonia affected cattle from England brought into Victoria. The disease soon spread throughout herds across Australia causing heavy losses.

1859   Rabbits introduced in Victoria soon spread to every state, devastating pastures.

1872   Cattle tick introduced from Java, soon spread throughout northern Australia causing redwater fever and killing millions of stock.

1876   Kelpie sheep dog bred at Wollonough and Hanging Rock stations.

1879   First use of artesian water, Kalara Station.

1880   First Australian freezing works, Victoria and Queensland, opened UK markets for frozen Australian beef.

1883–5   Cattle stations established in Kimberleys after enormous cattle drives by Duracks and others.

1898   First Australian-bred cattle developed: Illawarra shorthorns.

1910   Tick-resistant, heat-tolerant Brahman cattle introduced in northern Queensland.

1950s   Myxomatosis released as method to control rabbits.

1955   First road trains operated by the Farrell brothers in the Northern Territory. Within a decade road trains almost completely replaced droving in the outback.

THE SPREAD OF CATTLE

1788   First Fleet arrived in Australia with Cape cattle, brought from South Africa.

1791   Brahman bulls and cows introduced from India.

1792   Spanish-bred cattle from California arrived.

1794   First attempt to introduce English breeds of cattle (shorthorns, Herefords, Devons) resulted in all cattle dying.

1799   First successful introduction of English breeds.

1800   Devon bulls imported from England. A census of that year put the number of cattle in Australia at 1044. An indeterminate number, in the hundreds, were running wild beyond Cowpastures.

1806   3264 cattle in Australia.

1810   25 888 cattle in Australia.

1817   Governor Macquarie introduces the death penalty for stealing cattle.

1821   102 939 cattle in Australia.

1825   First registered English shorthorns in Australia.

1826   First registered Herefords in Australia.

1836   Governor Bourke allowed 'squatters' to graze stock on Crown Land on payment of a licence fee. The practice of squatting had by that time extended far beyond the government limits of settlement.

1898   First Australian bred cattle developed, Illawarra shorthorns.

1910   Tick-resistant, heat-tolerant Brahman cattle introduced in northern Queensland.

1926   Good performance of Zebu (Brahman)-Devon crossed cattle in northern Australia inspired development of the breed that would become known as the Droughtmaster.

1933   The first significant numbers of tick-resistant, tropical-climate-adapted Brahman cattle were introduced into Australia.

1951   Heat-hardy Santa Gertrudis introduced to Australia.

1982   Introduction of new Brahman bloodlines revolutionised the cattle industry in Northern Australia.

2013   Australian cattle herd (beef and dairy) numbered approximately 25 million.

VIKING

Published by the Penguin Group
Penguin Group (Australia)
707 Collins Street, Melbourne, Victoria 3008, Australia
(a division of Pearson Australia Group Pty Ltd)
Penguin Group (USA) Inc.
375 Hudson Street, New York, New York 10014, USA
Penguin Group (Canada)
90 Eglinton Avenue East, Suite 700, Toronto, Canada ON M4P 2Y3
(a division of Pearson Penguin Canada Inc.)
Penguin Books Ltd
80 Strand, London WC2R 0RL England
Penguin Ireland
25 St Stephen's Green, Dublin 2, Ireland
(a division of Penguin Books Ltd)
Penguin Books India Pvt Ltd
11 Community Centre, Panchsheel Park, New Delhi – 110 017, India
Penguin Group (NZ)
67 Apollo Drive, Rosedale, Auckland 0632, New Zealand
(a division of Pearson New Zealand Ltd)
Penguin Books (South Africa) (Pty) Ltd
Rosebank Office Park, Block D, 181 Jan Smuts Avenue, Parktown North,
Johannesburg, 2196, South Africa
Penguin (Beijing) Ltd
7F, Tower B, Jiaming Center, 27 East Third Ring Road North, Chaoyang
District, Beijing 100020, China

Penguin Books Ltd, Registered Offices: 80 Strand, London WC2R 0RL, England

First published by Penguin Group (Australia), 2013

10 9 8 7 6 5 4 3 2 1

Text copyright © Evan McHugh 2013

The moral right of the author has been asserted

Cover and text design by John Canty © Penguin Group (Australia)
Photography copyright as acknowledged
Typeset in 9/16 Caecilia by John Canty, Penguin Group (Australia)
Colour reproduction by Splitting Image Pty Ltd, Clayton, Victoria
Printed and bound in China by Everbest Printing Co Ltd

National Library of Australia
Cataloguing-in-Publication data:

McHugh, Evan.
The Stockmen / Evan McHugh.
ISBN: 9780670076260 (hbk.)
Stockmen--Australia.
Australia--History.

636.213092

penguin.com.au

Jacket image:
Courtesy of John Hay/Getty Images.

Case image:
Courtesy of Scott Bridle.

Endpaper images:
A horseman looks down 1800 mtres to a clearing in the geehi Valley
of the Australian Alps, called Wild Cow Flats, a favourite grazing
paddock for Brumbies, 1949.
(J. Fitzpatrick, National Archives of Australia, A1200,L11946)

Early morning muster on Yulgilbar Station, NSW, 2012.
(Matt Miegel)

Rounding up Herefords on the side of the road during a drought,
Canberra district, 1968.
(National Archives of Australia, A1500, K19486)

Mustering near Canberra, c.1960s.
(National Library of Australia, vn4591141, Australian Information Service)

Prelim images:
p.i Stockmen bringing fattened cattle down from summer pastures
in Victoria's High Country, 1966.
(Keith Byron, National Archives of Australia, A1200, L55198)

pp.ii–iii Stockman 'Cobbo' roping a calf on Nicholson Station, in the
Kimberley region of WA,1955. The greenhide rope used is hand-
made. The throw was successful.
(Percy Spiden, State Library Of Victoria, H2008.121/116)

pp. iv–v (Detail) *A break away!*, oil on canvas (137.3 x 167.8 cm),
1891, Tom Roberts (1856–1931), Corowa, New South Wales and
Melbourne, Victoria.
(Elder Bequest Fund 1899, Art Gallery of South Australia, Adelaide)

pp. vi–vii Head stockman Shane Templeton turning an adventurous
weaner back to the safety of herd, Lake Nash, Barkly Tableland,
Northern Territory, 2008.
(Scott Bridle)